THE Passion OF
Christ Is My Passion
FOR TRUTH

BUBBA

authorHOUSE®

AuthorHouse™
1663 Liberty Drive
Bloomington, IN 47403
www.authorhouse.com
Phone: 833-262-8899

Published by AuthorHouse 01/19/2021

ISBN: 978-1-6655-1304-3 (sc)
ISBN: 978-1-6655-1303-6 (e)

Library of Congress Control Number: 2021900626

Print information available on the last page.

New King James Version (NKJV)
Scripture taken from the New King James Version®. Copyright ©
1982 by Thomas Nelson. Used by permission. All rights reserved.

Scripture taken from the King James Version of the Bible.

Contents

Introduction

I first would like to make this very clear: I'm nothing more than an average man, but probably a little lower than most. I do not claim to have a high degree of intelligence concerning the Holy Scriptures. I have studied the Scriptures for many years. I have relied on my Father in Heaven only for the understanding of His Word.

The Word of God teaches us that if we knock, the door will be opened to us (Matthew 7:7–8). In the very beginning of my studies of Scripture, I did not understand one word of it. I realized, at that time, that I was a carnal man with a carnal mind. The problem was, how could I determine spiritual knowledge from the written carnal language of the Bible? I first had to recognize what was carnal and what was spiritual. Then I realized that what was carnal, many times, was literal truth but had a spiritual knowledge behind it all. My realizing this truth is when the picture of spiritual knowledge focused so well. I could then see the full picture of carnal language going to a carnal mind but producing spiritual knowledge. I know this might sound a little foreign to you, but after you've finished reading this book, you will understand the spiritual knowledge of the carnal language.

Quite often, as I'm reading Scripture, I put myself right there in the story with the characters. I have walked with Adam and Eve and our Lord in the Garden of Eden in the cool of the day. As I think about it now, I can feel the love of God. There was no stress, no worry, no pain, no sin in the world to bring us shame.

At that time, the world of Adam and Eve was as our Lord prayed in His teaching ministry for His disciples. He taught how to pray to our Father in Heaven, as Jesus prayed these words: "Thy kingdom come on Earth as it is in Heaven."

I suspect that many of us have read the Bible from Genesis to Revelation, and if not, then we still know of the stories and events within the books of the Bible. As Christians, we should realize that the world was perfect. We remember that God created Adam and Eve in His own perfect image. The Bible teaches that Adam and Eve had no sin. The world they lived in had no existence of sin. If they walked with God daily, they were in the light. The Bible teaches us that in the light, there is no darkness.

But darkness did come into the world. This is when Satan, God's adversary, tempted Adam and Eve, and they rebelled against God's Word by the temptation of Satan, just as adolescents will rebel against their parents to do their own will. This is because of sin in the world.

Many people of this world will rebel against the law—that is, man's law. Keep in mind, however, that man's law, in many cases, is the reflection of God's law—the Ten Commandments. But also keep in mind that we are imperfect beings, as men and women of this world. Our laws may be wishy-washy and too unstable to even be called *law*. Man will change laws to suit his purpose—or his pocketbook.

Here in Louisiana, at least in my lifetime, gambling was illegal. Legal gambling, however, dates back to the original US colonies. Gambling laws have been pushed forward or reversed for centuries throughout the world. In the United States, the laws concerning gambling have been altered or changed many times through the decades. In 1991, riverboats—in the beginning, a gambling boat—had to leave the shore and be in open waters for gambling to be legal. Then, eventually, the riverboats no longer had to leave the dock to operate legally. Gambling of some kind is everywhere.

Alcohol also once was illegal. During Prohibition in the United States, alcohol was illegal from January 17, 1920, until December 5, 1933. I am quite sure that sales tax on alcohol was the main factor for lawmakers of each state and for representatives of this country in legalizing alcohol.

At one time, abortion was also illegal. The following quotes about abortion come from Wikipedia:

> In 1970, Hawaii became the first state to legalize abortions on the request of the women, and New York repealed its 1830 law and allowed abortions up to the 24th week of pregnancy. Similar laws were soon passed in Alaska and Washington.
>
> Specifically, abortion is legal in all US states, and every state has at least one abortion clinic.

Roe versus Wade was a 1971–1973 landmark decision by the US Supreme Court. The court ruled that a state law banded abortions (except to save the life of the mother) was constitutional. The ruling made abortion legal in many circumstances.

In my opinion, abortion (with the exception of saving the life of the mother) and partial-birth abortion never should have been legal. My reasons for this are the many circumstances. What in God's creation could be more gravely important than to save the life of the mother? I cannot see any other circumstance that would justify taking the life of an unborn child. Many may disagree, but I can plainly see the many circumstances as the root of all evil: the love of money.

Since 1971, there have been millions of unborn babies killed in their mothers' wombs. I believe this is the most barbaric act of humankind. If you or someone you know has committed this most barbaric act of sin, I pray in the name of Jesus, as I beg you to come to Christ Jesus for the remission of sins. Jesus, from His passion as Christ, as the Tabernacle of God Himself, will renew you with a clean and pure history of life. It is the only way to salvation—by the blood of the Lamb of God. Making the decision to have an abortion had to have been some kind of understanding by a religious belief or perhaps none at all. One thing is certain: it did not come from a relationship with God.

Jesus said, "I am the light of the world. He who follows Me shall not walk in darkness, but have the light of life" (John 8:12).

Abortion once was illegal. Many things that were illegal are now either legal or just go unnoticed by the law, such as a man and a woman living in a common-law marriage. A question to Wikipedia—"Is common-law marriage legal in all fifty states?"—receives this answer:

> To be exact, as of 2020, only eight states still allow common-law marriages to be formed in them. ... However, all 50 states must recognize common-law marriage validly created in other states that allow them.

A common-law marriage, in God's law, is illegal; it is known as adultery. It also was illegal in man's law at one time. Why was it illegal? Because lawmakers were quite aware of God's law and that adultery was punishable by death, in God's judgment. The world we live in is still a sinful world and is getting worse. God's law never changes, and this is why He is coming back to set it straight and reclaim His world.

We might think that religion might help us regain our honor with God. How foolish can we be, for in many cases, religion shows no honor at all. What do I mean by this? Well, to my knowledge, for centuries, Catholics and Protestants in Great Britain and Ireland killed one another because of religious and political beliefs, and they read the same Bible.

> You shall love your neighbor as yourself.
> (Matthew 22:39)

If we would take the time to do the research on the history of religious beliefs, we would see that millions, perhaps billions, of deaths have been caused by the beliefs of a religion of some kind, whether Christian or non-Christian. Some satanic cults offer human sacrifice in their so-called religious rituals.

Look up the word *religion* in any dictionary. It will plainly tell you that religion is an organized belief system. Since the fall of Adam and Eve, religion of some kind has been responsible, in one way or another, for the death of billions. Remember Cain and Abel, the bloodshed of Abel, and the countless number of people killed in this world because of some understanding of religion? Even think of the great flood during Noah's time; these people were killed by God because of their disbelief. These points also may be considered a religious belief, but they are truly biblical facts.

During World War II, the Nazis killed millions of Jews, and other people as well, because of who they were or because of their religious beliefs. If you research all the so-called Christian religions in this country, you will see the dark side—there were many murders because of their religious beliefs.

Between the fifteenth and sixteenth centuries, the Aztec Indians offered human sacrifices because of their religious beliefs. Also, there is the story of Vlad Dracula, who was born in Romania in 1431 and died in December 1476. He was responsible for at least eighty thousand deaths and impaled many of his victims. He claimed to be a Roman Catholic. I do not believe he knew his religion or his God. Blind sin leads to this sort of thing, when we don't have knowledge of God's Word.

Think of the Egyptians and how many Jews they killed; also think of how many Egyptians God drowned during the parting of the Red Sea. Think of the many religions in the United States—many so-called Christian religions—that have committed murder and called it the will of God. Consider Ervil Morrell LeBaron (1925–1981), who was the leader of a Mormon fundamentalist group. He believed he had the right to kill many of his rivals, and he justified his actions by using a religious doctrine called *blood atonement*. This is ridiculous.

Think of Jonestown, with Jim Jones, who caused the death of nine hundred followers on November 18, 1978. Think of David Koresh in Waco, Texas, and the many lives lost there because of religious beliefs. I could go on and on with the dark history of religious belief causing the death of millions; it seems endless.

Why has this happened? We are not created in the perfect image of God, as were Adam and Eve in the beginning. Because of their sin, we are the offspring of sin. We are born dead to the Spirit of God. This is why Jesus said that unless one is born again, he will not see the kingdom of Heaven (John 3:1–21).

With that said, let me give you a spiritual picture—from the creation of Adam and Eve; to a fallen world, dead to the Spirit of God; to a reclaimed world, reconciled by God through Christ our Lord (2 Corinthians 5:17–21). From this carnal language of scripture, we may receive the spiritual knowledge of the Tabernacle of God Himself, as of the Son of God in all His Glory. I say this because it is the Father's Glory, and He will share His Glory with no one (Isaiah 42:8). With the truth of spiritual knowledge of all

Scripture, we can boldly see the all-loving, the all-merciful, the Almighty God, our Father in Heaven.

First things first. Picture the world as a big clock. Adam and Eve were created at twelve o'clock. They and the world were sinless. The beauty of God's light was His Glory that shone through the Heavens to the Earth. God truly loved His creation of humankind and the magnificent beauty of the world—all the planets, the beautiful stars, and all the galaxies. It truly was heaven, in a sense, on a planet known as Earth. This is how it was in the beginning with Adam and Eve, as they lived in a true relationship with God, our Father. They had no religion to worship Him. They had a relationship of love, honor, and trust by obeying God's Word.

This relationship was the true existence of love from God by His Word. In the beginning, Adam and Eve shared this love of God, our Father, by obeying His Word, but for true love, a choice had to be made. Do we love the Creator of all, or do we love to indulge in the lust of all creation?

We, as humans, now have the Word of God, the Bible, to learn the history of our existence. We once had a beautiful, loving relationship with our Father in Heaven, as we know from the lives of Adam and Eve. We also learn from the Word of God that because of the lust of creation, Adam and Eve lost this true value of love, and now, a choice must be made. This choice is the only true way to establish true love for God, which brings us 360 degrees around, back to twelve o'clock at the creation of Adam and Eve.

We have gone through hell with wars and death, sickness and religion, but God used religion to bring the knowledge of Him back into the world. From the one and only religion

God ever established, the Jewish religion, the knowledge of God was renewed in the world. Then, from that knowledge of religion came our Mediator, the Redeemer, the Savior, the Messiah, the Son of God, the Son of man, the Tabernacle of God Himself (Revelation 21:3).

Because of Him, Jesus, and all of the above, we now can have that true, loving relationship with our Father in Heaven. This, of course, is if we search and seek God diligently; then we will receive the spiritual knowledge of the carnal language.

We will then realize that we, as humankind, have traveled 360 degrees in our history of life on earth—from a perfect world, with a loving relationship with God, our Father, to a fallen world with the blindness of sin. Sin then infected us deeply with the many symptoms of religion. If you think not, just refresh your mind and emotions, and think deeply of September 11, 2001. Think of the horror in New York City as sin was manifested from the heartless black hole of the emptiness of religion. Do your own research; religion was the number-one factor why the World Trade Center's Twin Towers came down.

We, as Christians, children of God, are now approaching twelve o'clock, as we have almost completed the 360-degree mark. We have traveled through the history of life on earth in sin and in the darkness of many religions.

The time will soon come for the Church of God to regain that true love with our Father, with an intimate relationship, as Adam and Eve had in the beginning. We in this life on earth will soon come full circle. As Jesus prayed, "Your kingdom come. Your will be done on earth as it is in heaven" (Matthew 6:10). This kingdom will continue forever, for it will be by choice, not by command. This is true love, because God is love, and His love was completely expressed by the passion of Christ!

Praise be to God!

Acknowledgments

For the recognition of these people, their names will be placed on this page in this book, and this book will be placed in history for as long as our Lord will allow His Word to be preached. From the bottom of my heart, I thank each and every one of you.

For my wife, Vera Gayle Boutwell Traina, I thank you deeply. I believe God had a plan thirty-one years ago when He brought us together. If you had not been the woman you are, I am quite sure I would not be the man I am today. I thank you for putting up with me in my youth, as the troubled soul that I was, and for the time you have spent alone as I diligently sought greater knowledge of the Word of God. With all my love, I thank you for your patience, for I truly believe God has blessed you with His love. If you hadn't given me the time to seek the knowledge of God, then perhaps we both would still be living in darkness.

I wish to share my gratitude and thanks to Elizabeth Prestenback Majors, better known to all as Beth. She is a family member and a lifelong friend. She has helped me in the past and now, by proofreading my manuscript, looking for anything that must be corrected. I thank you, Beth, for your time, your concern, and your willing heart to learn another man's opinions. May God bless you. I pray in Jesus's name!

I also would like to mention my cousin Suzanne Brocato Miles, her daughter Bonnie Miles O'Daniel, and Bonnie's daughter Bentley Suzanne Bateman. I thank you, Bonnie, for the beautiful drawing of Jesus for the front cover of my book. Suzanne, I thank you and your granddaughter Bentley for encouraging Bonnie to draw the picture. It is truly a blessing for me. I pray that God, our Father in Heaven, will Bless every one of you with an abundance of His love.

I would like to express gratitude and thanks to my three sisters, Mary Jo Traina Nye, Toni Ann Traina, and Roselyn Marie Traina. For many years, I have gathered information concerning the Word of God. When I became the man I am in Christ Jesus, my concerns for my sisters grew to an all-time high. They are the last of my immediate family. I wanted to make sure they knew God as I know Him. Even though we were not always close because of busy lives and our living in different states, my concerns for their safety in Christ, and their families as well, drove me to write what God has given me. My love and concern grew for my entire family, both on my father's side and my mother's side. Then, it truly weighed on me, like a heavy burden, that everyone I had known in my life must know the truth of what God has given me.

Because I am a born-again Christian and a member of the body of Christ, it is my duty to share my thoughts and opinions. The Bible teaches us that love is the greatest gift of all (1 Corinthians 13:13). Without love for one another, I cannot see how anyone can feel secure about his or her safety in Christ Jesus. It is not how good we are that allows us to enter heaven, and it is not how bad we are that keeps us out of heaven; it's the lack of knowledge of our Lord Jesus and the true value of His love.

Though these people and others may not fully understand my opinions, we all can agree on one thing: Jesus Christ is our Lord and Savior (Isaiah 9:6).

Praise be to God!

Passion of Christ, Our Father's Love

T he anointed one, God's perfect image, is the Son of
God, the only begotten of our Father (Colossians 1:15).
In my interpretation of scripture, Jesus the man became
Jesus the Christ as the anointed one at His baptism. This is
when the Holy Spirit of God descended on Jesus like a dove
(John 1:32) and when the ministry of Jesus began, as well
as the mystery of the Church. The mystery of the Church
was still not known until more than three years after the
death, burial, and resurrection of Jesus, the Son of God.
The Church age began, as stated so well in Colossians 1:18:

> And He is the head of the body, the Church,
> who is the beginning, the firstborn from
> the dead, that in all things He may have
> the preeminence.

Preeminence means "surpassing all others; superiority."
Colossians 1:24–27 restates the truth of John 1:1:

> I now rejoice in my sufferings for you,
> and fill up in my flesh what is lacking in
> the afflictions of Christ, for the sake of

His body, which is the church. of which I became a minister according to the stewardship from God which was given to me for you, to fulfill the Word of God, the mystery which has been hidden from ages and from generations, but now has been revealed to His Saints. To them God willed to make known what are the riches of the glory of this mystery among the Gentiles: which is Christ in you, the hope of glory.

Also, Colossians 2:2 states "that their hearts may be encouraged, being knit together in love, and attaining to all riches of the full assurance of understanding, to the knowledge of the mystery of God, both of the Father and of Christ."

The mystery of the Church was not known until it was preached by Paul, the twelfth apostle, picked by Christ Himself. Saul, or Paul, as Christ named him, was chosen to replace Judas Iscariot after he had hanged himself. Matthias was first picked by the remaining eleven disciples. I first learned this information from a lady named Tee at a Bible study. Then, with further study, I plainly saw that Matthias was never mentioned as a disciple again. Jesus picked the first twelve, so why would He not pick the last, as the twelfth apostle would primarily preach to the Gentiles?

John 1:1 speaks clearly of the beginning of the Church age. It was a Jehovah's Witness who forced me to seek the truth of John 1:1. My friend, a man I worked with, told me that Jesus could not be God but only the Son of God. He quoted from my Bible: "In the beginning was the Word, and the Word was with God and the Word was God" (John 1:1). Then he said to me, "God had no beginning, and He has no end."

"Of course, I agree with you," I said. "God always was and will be."

"Well, how can John 1:1 have any truth when it states, 'In the beginning was the Word and the Word was with God and the Word was God'?"

"I don't know the answer just yet," I said. Then I thought, *The Bible will not contradict itself. This is carnal language filled with Spiritual knowledge.* I had not walked fifty feet from him when I heard from God. He explained to me that John 1:1 was the beginning of the Church age and that Christ was the beginning of the Church. Of all scripture, John 1:1 is complete in all Spiritual knowledge, as I will explain.

In the beginning was the Word—that is, God the Almighty, as the Holy Spirit, is the Word, for He spoke all things into existence by His Word. And the Word was with God, but the word *with* does not mean "alongside of" but "to be as one," not only in Spirit but in human form. And the Word was God—we all know Jesus as the Word of God. Why? John 3:34 states, "For He whom God has sent speaks the words of God, for God does not give the Spirit by measure." John1:1, in my opinion, clearly explains the mystery of the Church age. John the Baptist was preaching of the coming Messiah, the Son of God, the Tabernacle of God Himself (Revelation 21:3). The passion of Christ was the love of God Himself!

I feel that God speaks to each and every one of us at some time in our lives. Perhaps because of our decisions but mainly because of the way we live, it may be very brief or not noticed as the voice of God. Romans 10:17 states, "So then faith comes by hearing, and hearing by the Word of God."

I believe in my heart that the Word of God is the identity of God. Many of us will not understand this until we are born again. Jesus quotes this in John 3:3: "Most assuredly, I say to you, unless one is born again he cannot see the kingdom of God." I believe the reason we must be born again is that we are born spiritually dead to the Spirit of God. John 3:5–8 explains it so well:

> Jesus answered, "Most assuredly, I say to you, unless one is born of water and the Spirit, he cannot enter the kingdom of God. That which is born of the flesh is flesh, and that which is born of the Spirit is spirit. Do not marvel that I said to you, you must be born again. The wind blows where it wishes, and you hear the sounds of it, but cannot tell where it comes from and where it goes. So is everyone who is born of the Spirit."

Once we have received the Spirit of God, we are born again. We will hear from God personally as we read or hear His Word preached. Then, sometimes God will speak to us when we least expect it.

Many times, God will speak to me when I am driving. Sometimes, I may be speaking to Him first or be in prayer with Him, and then I will hear from Him. But not always. At times, He speaks first.

I can hear the voice of God, loud and clear, in my mind and heart. I have never heard an audible voice of God. As we come to know God as our Father in Heaven, we come to know one another as children of God, as we are the body of Christ as the Church. We will be joined together as one in spirit. We will testify or witness to the Word of God. Many will not understand if they have not received God's Spirit or haven't been born again. I can plainly see this truth in John 3:11:

> Most assuredly, I say to you, We speak what
> We know and testify what We have seen,
> and you do not receive Our witness.

Notice that in the New King James Version of John 3:11, the word *We* is capitalized, as is *Our*. This capitalization does not appear in the King James Version of 1611. Even so, I believe it is making a point. We are one in Christ, as Christ is one in the Father.

Jesus tells us in John 20:22, "Receive the Holy Spirit," or, as stated in 1 John 5:7, "For there are three that bear witness in Heaven: the Father, the Word, and the Holy Spirit; and these three are one."

As I understand scripture, the Father is a witness to Himself, and His earthly Tabernacle, His Son, Jesus, was a witness on Earth to the Father. In John 18:37, Jesus is quoted as saying, "For this cause I was born, and for this cause I have come into the world, that I should bear witness to the truth." We, as the church, are also witnesses of the Father from the knowledge of His Son, Jesus, His earthly Tabernacle. So who are the three who bear witness in Heaven as the Father and Son and Holy Spirit? In my opinion, it is the Father, the Holy Spirit; His earthly Tabernacle Jesus, who brought us His Word and the Holy Spirit; and, of course, the Church that has received His Holy Spirit. We are as one, in spirit.

Many may be lost because they refuse to pay attention to the voice of God, as they are distracted by such things as money, fame, and prestige in this world. They are lovers of pleasure, rather than lovers of God. The conclusion is found in 2 Timothy 3:4. Satan is a deceiver, and he will do anything he can to keep you from receiving the Spirit of God, our Father in Heaven. We are born dead to the Spirit of God. If this were not so, then Jesus would not have made the following statement in John 3:3:

> Jesus answered and said to him, "Most assuredly, I say to you, unless one is born again, he cannot see the kingdom of God."

Many of us will never pick up the Bible and read or—better yet—study it and find the many mysteries known only to the Church of God. The Church of God of which I speak refers to the saints of God, members of the body of Christ, who will read, study, and find the mysteries for themselves. Many of us, even in the Church, will not study or read the Bible to any measure. We will simply take words of belief from our so-called church leaders, such as priests or preachers. The priest, the preacher, and the saints of God who may be assembled there are the Church, not the building.

If they are correct in what they teach, then all may be well. But if not, your eternal life may be at stake. This is why it is so important to know Jesus Christ as our Lord, God, and Savior.

> He who believes in Him is not condemned, but he who does not believe is condemned already, because he has not believed in the name of the only begotten Son of God. (John 3:18)

Begotten of the flesh! Born of a woman! The Tabernacle of God Himself—Revelation 21:3 in any Christian Bible.

As a Saint of God who spends some time reading and studying Scripture, I have to ask, "Who is the Son of God?" My answer to that question is that the Son of God is Jesus. As Isaiah 9:6 tells us:

"For unto us a Child is born" (Jesus).

"Unto us a Son is given" (this would be the sacrificed Son of God).

"And the Government will be upon His shoulder" (this means He, Jesus, will have all power and authority).

"And His name will be called Wonderful, Counselor, Mighty God, Everlasting Father, Prince of peace" (which makes them both, of course, the Almighty invisible Holy Spirit, One God).

Isaiah 9:6 plainly states that Jesus is the Son of God, as well as the Father, God Himself. This verse fits perfectly well with Revelations 21:3 as a needed part of a jigsaw puzzle to see the plain truth in a picture of love. Revelation 21:3 states,

> And I heard a loud voice from Heaven saying, behold, the Tabernacle of God is with men, and He will dwell with them,

and they shall be His people. God Himself
will be with them and be their God.

This I see as the true passion of Christ. For as I see God,
I see Him as an all-loving God, an all-merciful God, an
Almighty God. Many Scriptures convinced me of just how
the One and True God has come as servant to teach us the
true value of the love of God.

Jesus said in John 5:43, "I have come in my Father's
name, and you do not receive Me; if another comes in his
own name, him you will receive." Again in this Scripture,
as well as many others, I truly believe Jesus is making a
statement. This would be to always identify the One and
True God. I believe that this is why we pray in the name
of Jesus. By quoting His name, we are identifying the One
and Only True God!

John 14:6–7 tells me this is truth as Jesus states,

I am the way, the truth, and the life. No
one comes to the Father except through
Me. If you had known Me, you would have
known My Father also; and from now on
you know Him and have seen Him.

Now, doesn't that Scripture sound like what Isaiah 9:6
tells us? This also proves to me what Jesus meant when He
said in John 10:30, "I and My Father are one."

Therefore, if anyone is in Christ, he is a
new creation; old things have passed away;
behold, all things have become new. Now
all things are of God, who has reconciled

us to Himself through Jesus Christ, and has given us the ministry of reconciliation, that is, that God was in Christ reconciling the world to Himself, not imputing their trespasses to them, and has committed to us the word of reconciliation. Now then, we are ambassadors for Christ, as though God were pleading through us: we implore you on Christ's behalf, be reconciled to God. For He made Him who knew no sin to be sin for us, that we might become the righteousness of God in Him. (2 Corinthians 5:17–21)

The passage in 2 Corinthians 5, above, shows me the love of God as Jesus Christ, the Son of God, and as Jesus Christ, the Tabernacle of God Himself. The Tabernacle of God or the Son of God was born of a virgin, the Virgin Mary. Matthew 1:23 states, "Behold, the virgin shall be with child, and bear a Son, and they shall call His name Immanuel," which is translated as "God with us."

Now, I pray that you will understand and not be offended by what I'm going to say. When I read Scripture, the words speak to me as they are written. But if I use church doctrine (an organized belief system of any denomination) to steer me in my understanding, I remain confused by some Scriptures, which sounds like a complete contradiction of truth. Whether I am right or wrong in my understanding of Scripture is not important to me at this time. I am writing and teaching what I believe is truth from the Holy Scriptures. If I am completely wrong, then God, my Holy

Father in Heaven, might tell me, as I stand before Him, just how foolish I am. Then, I am quite sure that if I were able to look around and see anyone from the Bema, or judgment seat, of Christ (see 1 Corinthians 3:12–15; also 2 Corinthians 5:10), I would see that I am not alone.

I am more than certain that I won't be the only one to hear those words; I'm sure it's the same with many others. I believe I am truly following Scripture. I would much rather have my God tell me how foolish I am than for Him to tell me, "I have shared every word of truth with you from the teachings of my only earthly Tabernacle, My only begotten Son, Jesus Christ, and you were ashamed to share it with others. Friend—how may I call you friend when you were afraid to preach, teach, or witness what I have given you? If I have given you the truth, why should you be ashamed or afraid to boldly speak the words I have given you? By this cause, you have no increase." These words, I do not want to hear!

> Do not lie to one another, since you have put off the old man with his deeds, and have put on the new man who is renewed in knowledge according to the image of Him who created him, where there is neither Greek nor Jew, circumcised nor uncircumcised, barbarian, Scythian, slave nor free, but Christ is all in all. (Colossians 3:9–11)

I believed the above scripture is telling us to be truthful about who we were before Christ came into our lives. Before the Holy Spirit dwelled in us, we were not who we are now. We are new creatures in Christ; we should boldly state our testimonies for the Glory of God.

We must patiently wait for the revelation of understanding from God Himself. Then and only then, all Scripture will fall into place like a big jigsaw puzzle, and then we will see that beautiful picture of love and truth.

Jesus told Pontius Pilate in John 18:37, "For this cause I was born and for this cause I have come into the world, that I should bear witness to the truth, everyone who is of the truth hears my voice." For some reason, I feel urged to emphasize this Scripture, in which Jesus, in my opinion, is fulfilling all Scripture as He speaks to Pilate. Pay close attention to the words:

> Pilate therefore said to Him, "Are You a king then?"
> Jesus answered, "You say rightly that I am a King." (John 18:37 KJV)

Jesus is answering Pilate as truthfully and justifiably as He possibly can at this time. For Jesus is King of Kings and Lord of lords. But at this time, He is the Tabernacle of God Himself, as the Son of God, the servant of God, who will die and pay the penalty of death for the forgiveness of sin. Jesus plainly changed the subject of Scripture and simply explained to Pilate why He had come into the world at that time. We can see this by His answer: "For this cause, I was born, and for this cause, I have come into the world, that I should bear witness to the truth. Everyone who is of the truth hears my voice."

I believe that when Jesus said, "I should bear witness to the truth," that He, as the Tabernacle of God or Son of God, was witnessing the very beginning of the mystery of the Church. Jesus, the man, was filled with the fullness of the Holy Spirit, God Himself, and John 1:14 and Revelation 21:3. Our Almighty Father God had to come as the Son of God to fulfill all Scripture and prophecy. God, our Father, as the Almighty Holy Spirit, came as the only begotten Son, begotten of the flesh, His earthly Tabernacle, for the opportunity to teach the Truth of Himself. As Jesus, the man, the world then and even now can clearly see His character as the never-ending, merciful love of God.

At this time. Jesus was a human, a man of flesh, filled with the fullness of the Almighty Spirit of God Himself. He came to His creation as the salvation of His creation. Jesus was indeed God's right-hand man, as the Son of God, as John 1:14 plainly states: "And the Word was made flesh and dwelt among us." Who is the Word? Of course, it's God, our Father, Himself, for He spoke the world and everything else into existence by His Word.

And we beheld His Glory, the Glory as the only begotten of the Father, full of grace and truth. How do I know this is truth? By Scripture, of course! Revelation 21:3 plainly states that Jesus, the Son of God, was indeed the Tabernacle of God Himself and the Word of God because of what John 3:34 states: "For He whom God has sent speaks the words of God, for God does not give the Spirit by measurer" (sent or to be born of the Blessed Virgin Mary). What is the difference, except word choice? The flesh man, vessel, or Tabernacle of God, Jesus, born of Mary, His earthly mother, did not always exist. It was a creation of the Holy Spirit. This is why I believe Luke 1:35, in the King James Version of the Bible from 1611, states these words:

> And the angel answered and said unto her, The Holy Ghost shall come upon thee, and the power of the Highest shall overshadow thee: therefore also that holy thing which shall be born of thee shall be called the Son of God.

The body is nothing but a container or vessel. The true identity of the flesh body or Tabernacle was the Holy Spirit. The Holy Spirit always did exist and had a supernatural vessel known as *Melchizedek*. This, of course, is my opinion, and I will boldly state it as biblical fact, backed up by Scripture. Please read Hebrews 7 and 8. If you cannot see the truth of my statement in those two chapters, then read the entire book of Hebrews.

I believe God has always had an earthly vehicle, or Tabernacle, of some kind. God walked on this planet Earth many times in the cool of the day with Adam and Eve. He had appeared to Moses and to Abraham. Melchizedek had to be the supernatural vessel of God Himself. Melchizedek was of human form but of the supernatural form, as always with God. Jesus was of human form but of flesh, in and of this physical world.

Before the foundation of the world, God created man in His own image. This is why Jesus has no beginning and no end as the Holy Spirit. It was the same with Melchizedek. This is what makes Jesus the Son of God, the Tabernacle of God Himself, God Almighty in the flesh.

I pray that we all may see the truth of the love of God from the following Scripture:

> Though I speak with the tongues of men and of angels, but have not love, I have become sounding brass or a clanging cymbal. And though I have the gift of prophecy, and understand all mysteries and all knowledge, and though I have all faith, so that I could remove mountains, but have not love, I am nothing. And though I bestow all my goods to feed the poor, and though I give my body to be burned, but have not love, it profits me nothing. Love suffers long and is kind; love does not envy; love does not parade itself, is not puffed up; does not behave rudely, does not seek its own, is not provoked, thinks no evil; does not rejoice in iniquity, but rejoices in the truth; bears all things, believes all things, hopes all things, endures all things. Love never fails. But whether there are prophecies, they will fail; whether there are tongues, they will cease; whether there is knowledge, it will vanish away. For we know in part and we prophesy in part. But when that which is perfect has come, then that which is in part will be done away. (1 Corinthians 13:1–10)

Yes, what a glorious day this will be, when we see the coming of our Lord Jesus Christ. He was the Word made flesh, the complete and fullness of love. He will fulfill all things, visible and invisible.

Praise be to God!

2

Passion of Christ

As I sit here in deep thought of that unmerciful day of suffering and death of our Lord Jesus, I am astonished by the knowledge of Scripture that reminds me of His love and mercy. It was the night of the Passover meal, commonly called the night of betrayal.

In Luke 22:27, Jesus says, "But who is greater, he who sits at the table, or he who serves? Is it not he who sits at the table? Yet I am among you as One who serves." I know in my heart, with all the knowledge of Scripture I can muster, that Jesus, the Son of God, is the Tabernacle of God Himself (Revelation 21:3), which makes Him the only begotten of flesh, His vessel, of His own creation. I know this in my mind and heart as truth by all Scripture, but I cannot comprehend the love of God. It is too great, too strong, and too magnificent as of this statement, the passion of Christ, which He, the God of all creation, actually endured.

When I think of my God in Heaven, I think of the creation of the world, the universe, the many plants, the many stars and galaxies, and the many mysteries of creation we are not aware of. I think of life itself in every form on this planet. I think of the creation of Heaven and the Angels as the Glory of God around His throne. But at first, I do not think of Him as One sitting at a table, ready and willing to serve.

Yes, it is true that Jesus the Christ was the anointed, created vessel who contained the fullness of God's Holy Spirit. He came as our Savior, or the servant, to reclaim the creation of the world. The truth of this is mentioned in the following passage from 2 Corinthians:

> Now all things are of God, who has reconciled us to Himself [*us*, the Church] through Jesus Christ, and has given us the ministry of reconciliation [*us*, the Church, teaching God's Word], that is, that God was in Christ reconciling the world to Himself [Christ was the Tabernacle of God Himself (Revelation 21:3)], not imputing their trespasses to them [not crediting or holding their sins accountable to them], and has committed to us the word of reconciliation [the authority to teach salvation through Christ]. Now then, we are ambassadors for Christ [we are representing Christ, as the Church]. (2 Corinthians 5:18–20)

It's as though God was pleading through us: we implore (we beg) you on Christ's behalf to be reconciled to God. (Come to God through the knowledge of Christ.)

This, of course, is my opinion, on how I see the Scriptures.

When we say *God Almighty*, we definitely acknowledge His power and authority, but do we think of His greatness as the power of His love? John 3:16 states, "For God so loved the world that He gave His only begotten Son, that whoever believes in Him should not perish but have everlasting life."

God's only begotten Son was Jesus the Christ, which means that He was the anointed One to contain the fullness of God's Spirit. God is a Spirit, and He may take any form or vessel He wills. He is known as the Holy Spirit, our Father. I know this as truth by all Scripture, and I can see just how Almighty, all-loving, and all-merciful He is. I know this is truth by John 1:14, which reads, "And the Word became flesh and dwelt among us, and we beheld His glory, the glory as of the only begotten of the Father, full of grace and truth" (NKJV). This, of course, would be the Father's Glory, the Creator of all. This is the way I see it.

The Scriptures show me, just how Almighty God is, as the Son of God. In Luke 22:15, Jesus says the most incredible statement of love that could ever be expressed. This is how the New King James Version records His words:

> Then He said to them, "With *fervent* desire
> I have desired to eat this Passover meal with
> you before I suffer."

Think about that statement; He speaks with *fervent* (passionate, intense, emotional, whole-hearted, eager, anxious, committed, dedicated) desire before He suffers. This is a statement of personal and deep love with great admiration for His disciples. This is the Almighty God, the God of creation, speaking. He is ready to give up His earthly life as mediator and as Redeemer so that all Scripture and prophecy is fulfilled. He expresses His excitement of love and emotions with a great desire before He suffers. This, of course, would have been the passion of Christ, His earthly Tabernacle (Revelation 21:3).

The pain and suffering and death by sin is paid in full by the pain and suffering and death of the love of God, the passion of Christ, as the Tabernacle of God Himself. I believe that we as Christians, with a love for God, cannot fully comprehend the full impact of the tragedy of that life, completely exhausted, as the passion of Christ, the love of God.

In the New King James Version, 1 Corinthians 6:20 states, "For you were bought at a price; therefore glorify God in your body and in your spirit, which are God's." This Scripture alone confirms, in my mind, as a Christian, that I should live for God. I know and realize the truth of Scripture, God Almighty, the Creator of all, freely gave His only earthly Tabernacle, the man Jesus, as the redemption of sin at the cross. Please read these Scriptures in your Bible: John 3:16, Isaiah 9:6, and Revelation 21:3.

As I sit here, bringing to mind the history of my life before Christ was in me (and I in Him), it is still hard for me to truly understand that depth of God's love. I think back to what I might consider my most sinful day, and I can visualize that day quite well. In my heart, however, that day is very dim, even completely dark in some areas. This day, among many, was God-given, perhaps days of life that were lost by the darkness of sin. What truly breaks my heart now is knowing that Christ saw me on His day of passion, as well as on many others.

I think now that He may have seen me as the drunken fool I was—boisterous, with loud, sinful words and actions and then perhaps laughing about the sinful things I'd said or done. When I think about the unmerciful day of torment and the unbearable pain and suffering He experienced before His death, it is beyond my ability to justify His actions for me. I can only feel the love of God. He saw me as a broken man, lost in sin and headed for hell. Yet He still loved me enough to suffer and die that way for me.

The passion of Christ is truly God's love. We know that God is love, but I thought I had a handle on the words *unconditional love*. I truly believe the measure of God's love is above my thoughts of unconditional love. I don't know how to explain God's love for the passion of Christ, except to say God is love, and He truly is an awesome God—I reserve the word *awesome* for my God. Each definition of the word *awesome* in the dictionary somehow identifies the character of God. For me, this is the only word needed to explain God's character.

Think about the unmerciful suffering, pain, and agony He took upon Himself for our salvation. But He expressed the joy of love with great, fervent desire. As mentioned above, He said in Luke 22:15, "With *fervent* desire I have desired to eat this Passover meal with you before I suffer."

Jesus also said, in John 15:15, "No longer do I call you servants, for a servant does not know what his master is doing; but I have called you friends, for all things that I heard from My Father I have made known to you."

The passion of Christ is the greatest statement of love the world has ever known or will ever know. I know this because Jesus said in John 19:30, "It is finished!" I believe that when Jesus said, "It is finished," He was saying that the penalty of sin, which is death, has been bought with a price. And it was a very expensive price—the life of the only begotten of flesh the world will ever know, the Son of God, the Tabernacle of God Himself in all His Glory. This, of course, would be the Father's Glory, for He came as man, as the Tabernacle of God Himself.

Scripture fulfills itself with truth, like a big jigsaw puzzle—the pure, clean, honest picture of truth. We see this with many Scriptures, such as 1 Timothy 3:16:

> And without controversy great is the mystery of godliness: God was manifested in the flesh, justified in the spirit, seen by Angels, preached among the Gentiles, believed on in the world, received up in glory.

This Scripture plainly tells me that our Father, the Almighty Holy Spirit, created the man Jesus, born of a virgin. The Scripture reads the *only begotten of the Father*. He is known as the Son of God, but He is also, as Revelation 21:3 states, the Tabernacle of God Himself.

In the book of Genesis, we read the genealogy of many people, starting with Adam and Eve. It tells us the history of who was begotten from whom. This history brings us to the birth of Jesus from His mother, the Virgin Mary, of the Jewish faith. But John 1:14 plainly tells us that Jesus was the only begotten of the Father, the Almighty Holy Spirit, the Word made flesh.

Who is the Word? Of course, it's God Almighty, our Father in Heaven. He spoke the world and everything else into existence with His Word. Who brought us His Word?

Of course, it was the Son of God, the Tabernacle of God Himself. John 3:34 states, "For He whom God has sent speaks the Words of God, for God does not give the Spirit by measure." Sent from Heaven, or born of the Virgin Mary? In my opinion, it makes no difference. Why? Because Jesus always existed in Heaven as the Holy Spirit, God Himself, but His only begotten Son, His only earthly Tabernacle, was born of a virgin.

He was here on earth, which meant He was sent in any way you wish to believe. Not having the Spirit *by measure*, in my opinion, means He was 100 percent God in a flesh vessel. I believe this because John 1:10 states, "He was in the world, and the world was made through Him, and the world did not know Him." I prefer the translation of John 1:10 as it is stated in the King James Version of the Bible: "He was in the world, and the world was made by Him, and the world knew Him not." When I read this, I emphasize the pronoun *Him*.

Many Scriptures convince me of my passion for truth. Here are just a few you may read in your Bible: Matthew 1:23, Isaiah 45:5, Deuteronomy 32:39, 1 Timothy 3:16, Isaiah 9:6, and Exodus 3:14.

God has come to His creation, the world, many times in supernatural form. The Bible states in Genesis 3:8 that the Lord walked with Adam and Eve in the garden of Eden in the cool of the day. At that time, Adam and Eve had no sin. Therefore, the world had no sin in its existence. They and the world shared in the existence of the Glory of God, just as we will one day. When sin came into the world, there was then also darkness.

The Bible states in Exodus 33 that our Lord appeared to Moses, and Moses asked to see the face of God.

> But He said, "You cannot see My face for no man shall see Me, and live." And the Lord God said, "Here is a place by Me, and you shall stand on the rock. So it shall be, while My Glory passes by, that I will put you in the cleft of the rock, and will cover you with My hand while I pass. Then I will take away My hand and you shall see My back; but My face shall not be seen." (Exodus 33:20–23)

This too was a supernatural vessel, centuries before Jesus was born. It wasn't time to see the face of God, which would have been too intimate at that time. Why? The Tabernacle of God, Jesus, all Scripture, and all prophecy before the birth of Christ had not yet been fulfilled. The Bible also teaches in Genesis 18:1–4 that Abraham spoke with our Lord and two angels on the night Sodom and Gomorrah were destroyed.

The Lord had come to speak with Abraham concerning the promised son Isaac. The Bible does not say that Abraham actually saw the face of our Lord. This too was a supernatural vessel of God Himself. Hebrews 7:1–4 speaks of Melchizedek:

> For this Melchizedek, king of Salem, priest of the most high God, who met Abraham returning from the slaughter of the Kings and blessed him, to whom also Abraham gave a Part of all, first being translated

"king of righteousness," and then also
king of Salem, meaning "king of peace,"
without father, without mother, without
genealogy, having neither beginning of
days, nor ending of days, but made like the
Son of God, remains a priest continually.
now consider how great this man was, to
whom even the patriarch Abraham gave a
tenth of the spoils.

Does this indicate that he also may have been a
supernatural vessel of God Himself? The Bible does not
state that as an outright fact, but it does explain it as a
matter of facts—at least I think it does. If Melchizedek
were a supernatural vessel of God, perhaps he wore a veil
to conceal the Glory of God, not to be seen by men. I am
speculating, but the Scriptures do speak as facts. Perhaps
only his supernatural vessel, or Tabernacle, made like the
Son of God, could be seen. This, to me, would symbolize
the veil in the Jewish temple, separating it from the Holy of
Holies. But Jesus was born centuries later and was the only
earthly vessel, or Tabernacle, ever to be born on earth. He
was the only begotten of the flesh, the Son of God, Jesus
the Christ, the anointed One, the Word made flesh, the
passion of God's expression of the love and mercy He has
for His creation.

I am the Lord, and there is none else, there
is no God beside me; I girded thee [though
I have prepared you with great knowledge],

though thou hast not known me. (Isaiah 45:5 KJV)

One Lord, one faith, one baptism, one God and Father of all, who is above all, and through all, and in you all. (Ephesians 4:5–6 KJV)

But you, O Lord, are a God of full compassion, and glorious, long- suffering and abundant in mercy and truth. (Psalm 86:15)

But God, who is rich in mercy, because of His great love with which He loved us, even when we were dead in trespasses, made us alive together with Christ (by grace you have been saved). (Ephesians 2:4–5)

Therefore, be merciful, just as your Father also is merciful. (Luke 6:36)

He will again have compassion on us, And will subdue our iniquities. You will cast all our sins into the depths of the sea. (Micah 7:19)

God in Heaven is all-loving, all-merciful, and truly Almighty.

For God so loved the world that He gave His only begotten Son, that whosoever believes in Him should not perish but have everlasting life. (John 3:16)

I believe with my passion of love that my God, my Father in Heaven, did all these things. For He is love beyond measure. I can see He has a great love for His creation, a love that is expressed with great value. The passion of Christ truly shows us the precious value of His love as our Father— the Almighty, invisible God—in the physical, earthly man Jesus, who was the Tabernacle of God. He is with men, and He will dwell with them, and they shall be His people. God Himself will be with them and be their God (Revelation 21:3).

Praise be to my Lord, my God, my Savior, in Jesus's name!

3

From the Cross Was His Statement of Love; from His Throne Is His Judgment

I believe, from the passion of Christ and His resulting death on the cross, that God gave the world all the mercy within Him. This would be the forgiveness of sin by His death, burial, resurrection, and His loving grace.

> He who believes in Him is not condemned;
> but he who does not believe is condemned
> already, because he has not believed in the
> name of the only begotten Son of God.
> (John 3:18)

God is an all-loving, all-merciful God. He is also an all-righteous God. For God to be all in all, He must pass judgment when judgment is due, whether for life everlasting or eternal damnation. God is a loving God. He does not want to see anyone face eternal damnation, but we make choices in life; therefore, we make the decisions of where we will spend eternity.

There are only two choices that we can make. We can choose life—this is God's will; or we can choose death—this is our will to fulfill all the desires of the lust of the flesh, never thinking of the passion of Christ and what He did for us. Knowing what Christ did for us will lead us away from the choice of death. Jesus said in John 8:12, "I am the light of the world. He who follows Me shall not walk in darkness, but have the light of life."

From the life of Jesus, we can learn to see His light, which is the knowledge of God. Then we can live in the will of God. Without the light of Jesus, we live in darkness, which leads us to destruction and eternal damnation. We must search for His truth, for *His truth will make us free.* This, of course, would be free of sin and the penalty of death.

Some may disagree, which is their God-given right, but I will explain my understanding of destruction and eternal damnation by the choices they have made in life.

> Blessed and holy is he who has part in the first resurrection. Over such the second death has no power, but they shall be priests of God and of Christ, and shall reign with Him 1000 years. (Revelation 20:6)

Notice that verse 6 reads "of God and of Christ," but then it reads "and shall reign with Him"—singular, One God. This is no different than when we read "God and the Father," which can be found in James 1:27, as well as many other Scriptures. This is carnal language with spiritual knowledge. It simply means they are One and the same. Isaiah 9:6 explains the truth of it all quite well.

Now when the thousand years have expired, Satan will be released from his prison and will go out to deceive the nations which are in the four corners of the earth, Gog, and Magog, to gather them together to battle, whose number is, as the sand of the sea. They went up on the breath of the earth and surrounded the camp of the saints and the beloved city. And fire came down from God out of heaven, and devoured them. The devil, who deceived them, was cast into the lake of fire and brimstone, where the beast and the false prophets are. And they will be tormented day and night forever and ever. Then I saw a great white throne and Him who sat on it, whose face the Earth and the Heaven fled away. And there was found no place for them. And I saw the dead, small and great, standing before God, and books were opened. And another book was opened, which is the book of life. And the dead were judged according to their works, by the things which were written in the books. The sea gave up the dead who were in it, and Death and Hades delivered up the dead who were in them. And they were judged, each one according to his works. Then the Death and Hades were cast into the lake of fire. This is the second death. And anyone not found written in the

> Book of Life was cast into the lake of fire .
> (Revelation 20:7–15)

This, of course, is the judgment of Sinners. We must remember that we are all sinners, being born of the natural.

> Jesus answered and said to him, "Most assuredly, I say to you, unless one is born again, he cannot see the kingdom of God."
> (John 3:3)

This is why it is so very important for us to know Christ as the light of the world and to live for Him. Jesus is the only light in this dark world to lead us to the path of salvation. Trust in Jesus; without Him, we are truly blind to the righteousness of God.

It is also important for us, as Christians, as the Saints of God, to know that we will also stand before a judgment. This is not a judgment for salvation; we are already saved by realizing the passion of Christ and what He has done for us. We are saved by His loving grace. There is nothing we can do by our works to earn salvation. Love is the answer to salvation. By the light of Jesus, the Tabernacle of God Himself, we learn to freely give our lives to Him in this life, as He, as the passion of Christ, freely gave His earthly life for us. This is *true* love, not commandments written on stone or rules and regulations to live by. We, as Christians, in a relationship with God, freely live our lives with love for Him, freely given in return, for the love He expressed for us with His passion of Christ, as the Son of God.

> For God so loved the world that He gave
> His only begotten Son, that whosoever
> believes in Him should not perish but have
> everlasting life. (John 3:16)

We must realize by Scripture that His "only begotten Son" was His only fleshly Tabernacle ever. But God has been here many times in supernatural form. As we contain a portion of the Holy Spirit in our fleshly vessels—our Tabernacles, our bodies—the anointed One, Christ Jesus, contained 100 percent of the Spirit of God, which made Him God in the flesh. This truly gives me a clear understanding of the love of God as the all-loving, all-merciful, Almighty God, as the passion of Christ! This is an unexplainable love shown by the One and only God, Creator of all, my Father in Heaven.

The judgment we will stand for is the judgment of our love, by our works in Christ. These works are not works for salvation but our works for the righteousness of God, in the Glory of God and for the Glory of God.

> If anyone's work is burned, he [or she] will
> suffer loss; but he himself [or she herself]
> will be saved, yet so as through fire. (1
> Corinthians 3:15).

Using myself as an example, here's what I believe this Scripture teaches us: If I write my books in the hope of becoming famous or making a great deal of money, or I just believe that these words are coming from me, then it is all in vain. These works would be burned in the fire.

In ancient Rome and Greece, when any athletic sport was held, the judges always sat where they could accurately judge the outcome of the competition. Those seats were known in the Greek language as the *bema seats*. The bema seats, which might have been nothing more than large stones to sit or stand on, were placed in such a way that judges could justify every movement. The word *bema* is translated in English as "righteousness in judgment" or "judgment seat."

Matthew 27:19 speaks of Pontius Pilate, the fifth governor of the Roman province of Judea:

> While he was sitting on the judgment seat, his wife sent for him, saying, "Have nothing to do with that just Man, for I have suffered many things today, in a dream because of Him."

If this verse were written in ancient Greek, the word *judgment* would be *bema*. This is the judgment that we, as the Saints of God, will go through. It is known as the "judgment seat of Christ" in Romans 14:10, but many Christians will call it the bema seat of Christ—it means the same thing.

We will be judged for all our works but not for salvation; for works only.

> According to the grace of God which was given to me, as a wise master builder I have laid the foundation, and another builds on it. But let each one heed how he built on it. For no other foundation can

anyone lay than that which is laid, which is Jesus Christ. Now anyone build on this foundation with gold, silver, precious stones, wood, hay, straw, each one's work will become clear; for the Day will declare it, because it will be revealed by fire; and the fire will test each one's work, of what sort it is. If one's work which he has built on it endures, he will receive a reward. If anyone's work is burned, he will suffer loss, but he himself [or she herself] will be saved, yet so as through fire. (1 Corinthians 3:10–15)

I see the judgment of Christ for the Saints of God (or, as many claim, the bema seat judgment) as a recorded statement of true love. I believe God will measure the value of that love from the heart of the work given by the Saint of God. If the Saint's works are flawless and pure, without any self-gratification, then that Saint will receive a crown from the Lord. I believe that this will give us the authority to rule in some way in the New kingdom on Earth. As we new Saints receive these crowns, we will cast them back at the feet of Christ, for He is King of Kings and Lord of Lords, and this is the way we will submit to that knowledge, starting with the twenty-four elders.

And when the Chief Shepherd appears, you will receive the crown of glory that does not fade away. (1 Peter 5:4)

> Behold, I am coming quickly! Hold fast
> what you have, that no one may take your
> crown. (Revelation 3:11)

I've used the two Scriptures, above, only to show that we will receive crowns. There are many more Scriptures like these.

I believe with all my heart that when we see in our minds and hearts the one and true God, in all His Glory, at the cross, then we will truly know His love. When we can fully realize that the Creator of all has stepped down from His throne and came as a servant to His creation, the Earth, as the Son of God, in all His Glory, we will truly know His love! When we fully realize that the passion of Christ was endured by the Creator of all, then we can trust and accept His judgment.

Praise be to God, our Father in Heaven!

4

My Passion, with Love, from the Passion of Love, Christ Jesus

How can I express my love and concern for the people of this world? I am only a man—but I am not just a man! I am a Saint of God, a born-again Christian. The Spirit of Christ dwells within me, a portion of the Holy Spirit. The Holy Spirit is the Spirit of God, which is the Spirit of love.

In my younger years, I was blessed with the opportunity to travel to many different countries. Whether during my time in the army or my time working as a welder, I was always on the move to somewhere. Here in the United States, I have worked in just about every state on the East Coast. I have worked in many other states as well, including Washington State, as well as Vancouver, Canada.

Whether I traveled north or south of America or to Europe or the Middle East or even to China, people were always good to me. In general, people were friendly and willing to share their time with a complete stranger, a foreigner in a strange land.

Even before I was the man in Christ that I am today, people always intrigued me with their thoughts of life and their customs. Most of all, I was intrigued by their beliefs of God.

When people meet in foreign countries and cannot speak the same language, it's difficult to communicate with a solid understanding. When I was in a foreign country, I made it a priority to visit the temples of worship. At that time in my life, I thought it would give me a better understanding of how the people viewed the acknowledgment of God or gods. To my disappointment, it was always the acknowledgment of religion. It was always a geographical, organized belief system.

In some of the strange places I visited, human sacrifices were offered to a god of who-knows-what belief. As I stood in the Roman Colosseum, I visualized the many lives that were taken, just for the sport of it, and it broke my heart. *Why?* Because today, I am a new creature in Christ. Today, I can clearly see the mistakes of yesterday. I think that yesterday is gone, tomorrow may not come, and today is the day of salvation—if we come to Christ. In my opinion, the people of the world, for centuries now, have been blinded from the true identity of God, mainly because of religion inside and outside of Christianity, which is an organized belief system.

This world is a beautiful creation of God, but because of sin and the lack of knowledge of the one and true identity of God, many will not see the Glory in God's creation. I have met many people around the globe. I have witnessed many worshipping in the temples of whatever their belief in what they considered God or gods. Whether it was Judaism, Buddhism, Islam, Hinduism, or Christianity, the people were always sincere and diligent in their beliefs.

I still can see, clearly in my mind, the many young people kneeling in prayer before a statute of Buddha; I stood behind them, thinking of Christ Jesus. I still can hear the words of a middle-aged Muslim man as he knelt down toward the East and prayed to Allah, his god. This man was the captain of the crew boat that would bring me out on the Mediterranean Sea to get aboard a ship to do my job. As I patiently waited for this man, I thought of Christ Jesus.

When I visited the Vatican in Rome, I was amazed by the beauty of the artwork inside and the magnificent beauty of the architectural design of the building itself. As I stood inside the Vatican, I also thought of the cost of that building and the purpose of what it was meant to be. I don't know what the actual cost was when it was built, but information I found online suggests that today, it would probably cost about $8.2 billion. Think about that! It is just a building, but its purpose was to be a church. All that money and time in building it and the beauty of it all, and it is still not a church. It is a building, where the Saints of God, or the Church of Christ, may assemble.

As I think now of the magnificent beauty of it, I also think of Christ Jesus, nailed to a cross, with hardly any clothing. I think of the ugly actions of sin—sin that unmercifully had beaten the bloody body of Christ Jesus and then nailed it to a cross. I think of the price Christ Jesus paid for the Church. Christ was the beginning of the Church and paid for it with His life. For a greater understanding of what I just said, please read Colossians 1.

I will quote verse 18 and verse 24, so that we may see the truth of Scripture.

And He is the head of the body, the Church, who is the beginning, the firstborn from the dead, that in all things He may have the preeminence. (Colossians 1:18).

I now rejoice in my sufferings for you, and fill up in my flesh what is lacking in the afflictions of Christ, for the sake of His body, which is the Church. (Colossians 1:24)

Please take the time to read the first chapter of Colossians. Also, please keep in mind that Jesus Christ, the Son of God, was also the Tabernacle of God Himself (Revelation 21:3).

Today, we Christians may not think of Christ Jesus as the Church. Many of us will still visualize a great monument of beauty with a high steeple, perhaps painted white to symbolize the Glory of God as the Church. It doesn't matter what it looks like; it is still only a building. We, the Church of God, may go to any building and assemble as the Church. We don't go to church; we are the Church.

Jesus said in Matthew 18:20, "For where two or three are gathered together in My name, I am there in the midst of them" (KJV). Why is He in the middle? In my opinion, it is because Jesus is the Church, and we are in Him, as He is in us. We are the body of Christ.

Colossians 1:22 states, "In the body of His flesh through death, to present you holy, and blameless, and above reproach in His sight" (NKJV). I see this scripture in only one way: our Father in Heaven will see us here on Earth, as flesh but filled with His Spirit, as the Church, as the perfect, sinless body of Christ Jesus.

Do we know who we are as the Church? Do we realize what Christ Jesus lived through on that day of His passion, for the love of His Church? It was a mystery at that time, one unknown to the world.

As the Church, we live in a very special time. As the Saints of God, we are unique people, or souls of the Church age, the now-known mystery of the passion of Christ. Because of His passion for us, our hearts, like Christ Jesus's, should be open and bursting with love for one another, with a passion of hope that none would be lost.

I can say these words sincerely because of my travels around the world. I can still see the faces of many people who have no names—I only remember their faces and their knowledge of God or gods. I knew then that they did not know my God; they did not know Jesus Christ or anything about the Holy Spirit. I could feel only pity for them. Still, I didn't know very much about my God myself, so how could I have possibly helped them?

I pray now that my God, my Father in Heaven, has forgiven me. I believe it is so, only because of what Christ Jesus, the Son of God, the Tabernacle of God Himself, did for all of us.

Quite often, I think that if I had known then what I know now, I could have planted many seeds of life in the hearts of many people as I traveled the world. At that time, however, at least for the most part, I was filled with the desires of this world—the self-gratification of the flesh. I felt pity for many people of the world, not realizing that Jesus, the Lamb of God, the Tabernacle of God Himself, had pity on me—with a fervent desire of love, enough to save me from my sinful self, by His loving Grace.

Praise be to God, my Father in Heaven!

5

What Is Truth?

> Jesus said to them, I am the way, the truth, and the
> life. No one comes to the Father except through Me.
> —John 14:6

I consider these words from Jesus to be the most accurate truth, but they are misunderstood by many Christians. Jesus said,

> If you had known Me, you would have
> known My Father also; and from now on
> you know Him and have seen Him. (John
> 14:7)

In John 14:8, Philip asks Jesus to show them the Father. In John 14:9, Jesus plainly tells Philip, "He who has seen Me has seen the Father; so how can you say, 'show us the Father'?" I believe that John 14:10 is a very important scripture to understand, as it states, "Do you not believe that I am in the Father, and the Father in Me? The words that I speak to you I do not speak on My own authority; but the Father who dwells in Me does the works." This Scripture explains that Jesus, the Son of God, is the only earthly, or fleshly, Tabernacle of God Himself—the only Tabernacle begotten of the Father and born of a virgin, the Virgin Mary.

It's my opinion that this was the only earthly Tabernacle that God ever entered, and it was for the church age, the mystery of the Church. God, our Father, the Almighty Holy Spirit, and Jesus, the man, were One, as body and Spirit, in this physical world. That will explain why no one comes to the Father except through Jesus. Also, Jesus plainly states in John 10:30, "I and my Father are One." This means only one thing: He is the Almighty Holy Spirit!

Please read Colossians 2:9, John 3:34, Isaiah 9:6, John 1:14, 1 Timothy 3:16, and Revelation 21:3. I pray that after reading these Scriptures, you will see why no one comes to the Father except through Jesus. In my opinion, He is the Father, Son, and Holy Spirit as One. Please read Isaiah 9:6 again very carefully. That Scripture plainly states one person, or entity. This, of course, would be the Almighty Holy Spirit.

In the so-called Christian religion, there are many denominations. I am sorry to say these words, but Christianity is not a religion; it is an intimate relationship with our Father in Heaven, just as Adam and Eve had in the beginning. Adam and Eve did not have a religion to worship our Father.

John 4:24 states, "God is Spirit, and those who worship Him must worship in spirit and truth." This Scripture plainly tells me that true worship is in living every day in the Spirit of Christ and in the truth of His Word. Let me reiterate: this is not a religion but a relationship with our Father in Heaven, for we are all one in spirit.

I can plainly see how God introduced Himself back into the world by a religion. The Scriptures teach us that God brought Abram out from among his people, and God introduced Himself as the One and true God. Also at that time, God changed Abram's name to Abraham. Then, many years after Abraham, Isaac, and Jacob, the Jewish bloodline and its faith as religion was fully established. We all know from the words of the Bible that the Jewish Messiah, or the Son of God, our Savior, came from within that religion.

I believe we know our Father intimately from His earthly Tabernacle, Jesus the Christ. He is bringing us full circle, from relationship to religion, and eventually back to the relationship, as Adam and Eve had before they fell into sin. I can plainly see this truth by the following Scriptures:

> The woman said to Him, "Sir, I perceive that You are a prophet. Our fathers worshiped on this mountain, and you Jews say that in Jerusalem is the place where one ought to worship." Jesus said to her, "woman, believe Me, the hour is coming when you will neither on this mountain, nor in Jerusalem, worship the Father. You worship what you do not know; we know what we worship, for salvation is of the Jews."

In verse 23, Jesus is plainly stating a new beginning, which would be the New Testament. We know that our bodies are the Temples of the Holy Spirit. As the Christian Church, we have a unique way of worship, an intimate relationship with God our Father, as Adam and Eve had before they fell into sin. John 4:23 plainly tells me this is truth, as it states, "But the hour is coming, and now is, when the true worshipers will worship the Father in spirit and truth; for the Father is seeking such to worship Him." This Scripture tells me that we worship from the heart with an abundance of love, not from rituals, rules, and regulations, which is religion.

> For you are all sons of God through faith in Christ Jesus. For as many of you as were baptized into Christ have put on Christ. There is neither Jew nor Greek, there is neither slave nor free, there is neither male nor female; for you are all one in Christ Jesus. (Galatians 3:26–28)

As Christians today, we are so carnally minded. We will read Scripture with a carnal understanding and knowledge because we live in this physical world, and we think as physical or carnal beings. We will read carnal words to the carnal mind, but we are searching for spiritual knowledge and understanding.

The only way to receive spiritual knowledge and understanding is to bring all Scripture together in your mind, like a big jigsaw puzzle. Spread the Scriptures around so that you can see them clearly. Start to place them together to get a true picture of what the Bible teaches. Each Scripture must perfectly fit with the others. If all Scripture does not perfectly fit together, then something is wrong with your Bible translation. Or perhaps someone is teaching you carnal understanding and not spiritual knowledge. Regardless, I believe if we search Scripture for ourselves, God will give us revelation in all understanding.

Consider this example: the gospel of Matthew 3:17 states, "And suddenly a voice came from heaven, saying, 'This is My beloved Son, in whom I am well pleased.'" This verse is literal truth, but in my mind, it is also carnal understanding—but still truth! The problem, however, is that it is only half the story in carnal understanding. With spiritual knowledge as well, we will get the full story, or the true picture, of what all Scripture is telling us.

I believe the voice from Heaven was God, our Father. We must remember that God is Spirit, and He is everywhere at the same time. He is definitely in America and in every country on Earth. Yet also remember that He is on His throne in Heaven. With that said, let me explain Matthew 3:17 in the way I believe God explained it to me in all Scripture.

My thoughts: *This is my beloved Son in whom I am well pleased, for now I can come to my creation as my creation, man, Jesus (Revelation 21:3), the Tabernacle of God Himself, for the salvation of My creation. I can come as Mediator, as Redeemer, and fulfill all Scripture and Prophecy. I am so well pleased.*

I believe this wholeheartedly because of the following Scriptures:

> One Lord, one faith, one baptism. One God and Father of all, who is above all, and through all, and in you all. (Ephesians 4:5–6 KJV)
>
> I am the Lord, and there is none else, there is no God beside me; I girded thee,

though thou hast not known me. (Isaiah 45:5 KJV)

Now see that I, even I, am He, And there is no God besides Me; I kill and I make alive; I wound and I heal; Nor is there any who can deliver from My hand. (Deuteronomy 32:39)

Who has performed and done it, Calling the generations from the beginning? I, the Lord, am the first; And with the last I am He. (Isaiah 41:4)

I am the Lord, that is my name; And My glory I will not give to another. (Isaiah 42:8)

Jesus said, "I and My Father are one." (John 10:30)

Remember Ephesians 4:5—"One Lord, one faith, one baptism." I truly believe those words, as well as these from Isaiah 42:8—"And My glory I will not give to another."

I pray that we, as Christians, as one body united from all denominations, will one day see the big picture of that jigsaw puzzle of Scripture. I pray that we all will see the picture of true love expressed by the passion of Christ, the One and only God of creation, our Father of Heaven and of the New Kingdom on Earth, as it is in Heaven, as it is to come! I pray in Jesus's name, for He identifies my God, the One and Only.

Praise God!

6

How Can We Not
See Him as the Father?

Please understand that I did not write the words in this chapter to offend anyone because of their religious beliefs. I have not written these words to please or displease anyone. I am simply writing from my heart and what the Scriptures say to me.

I have been a believer in Christ Jesus all of my life, but I didn't get to know Him until more than thirty-five years ago. That was when I began to study Scripture. I am now sixty-nine. I don't claim to be a Bible scholar or anything close to that. I am just a man with a passion for truth.

I don't belong to any so-called Church. I left all of the so-called Christian Churches more than thirty-five years ago. It is not that I don't like them; I have love for all of them because I know Christ Jesus is in all of them. Jesus said in Matthew 18:20, "For where two or three are gathered together in my name, there am I in the midst of them" (KJV). By this Scripture alone, I believe that Christ is present in all so-called Christian Churches.

I believe that the difference has to do with the Saints of God themselves in Christ. This, of course, is in only our Father's knowledge. In this world, there is no one and not anything that is perfect, so I don't look for the perfect Church.

I will not sign up as a bona fide member of any denomination because there is none with which I can totally agree. If I were a member of any Christian denomination and spoke my heart concerning Scripture, I probably would be asked to leave. Why? Because I just don't see things in the way that many do in their organized belief systems. I don't say this as a negative statement against the people of many so-called Christian Churches. I state this as a matter of fact only.

For that reason alone, I wrote this chapter: "How Can We Not See Him as the Father?" In the title of this chapter, the pronoun *Him* refers to Jesus, the Son of God. Also, in the title is the noun *Father*; this refers to God Himself.

Whether you're confused or know where I'm going with this, please read this chapter. If for no other reason, do it for the love of God.

History plays a big part in the knowledge of the world. History is the primary factor in all ancient religions of today. Without the knowledge of history, ancient religions would have no format for their foundations; that is, is no evidence of their beliefs. Sometimes when we search for knowledge in history concerning religion—religion of any kind—some areas can be gray. Some ancient quotes from history may not quite line up with what we teach today. Here are a few quotes (found on Wikipedia) with regard to the Trinity:

> The first defense of the doctrine of the Trinity was in the early third century by

the early church father Tertullian. He explicitly defined the Trinity as Father, Son, and Holy Spirit and defended his theology against "Praxeas," though he noted that the majority of the believers in his day found issue with his doctrine.

Tertullian has been called "the Father of Latin Christianity" and "the founder of Western theology." Unlike many church fathers, Tertullian was never recognized as a Saint by the Eastern or Western Catholic tradition Churches."

I must add that any true believer in Christ Jesus, from any known so-called Christian Church, is a Saint of God. They are members of the body of Christ.

The following are scriptures from the New King James Version of the Bible on the subject of saints of God and we Christians as the body of Christ:

> Sing praise to the Lord, you saints of His, and give thanks at the remembrance of His Holy name. (Psalm 30:4)
> For God is not the author of confusion but of peace, as in all the churches of the saints. (1 Corinthians 14:33)
> So we being many, are one body in Christ, and individually members of one another. (Romans 12:5)
> For as the body is one and has many members, but all the members of that one

body, being many, are one body, so also is Christ. (1 Corinthians 12:12)

And He is the head of the body, the church, who is the beginning, the firstborn from the dead, that in all things He may have the preeminence. (Colossians 1:18)

With these few scriptures—and there are many more—it's plain to see that it does not matter what the Catholic Church recognized or did not recognize. If Tertullian was truly saved as a child of God, he was a saint and a part of the body of Christ as a member of the Church. Wikipedia provides the following information:

Praxeas was a Monarchian from Asia Minor who lived in the end of the 2nd century and the beginning of the 3rd century. He believed in the unity of the Godhead and vehemently disagreed with any attempt at the division of the personalities or personages of the Father Son and Holy Spirit in the Christian Church.

Whether the early Church fathers believed in the Trinity, is a subject for debate. Some of the evidence used to support an early belief in the Trinity are tragic statements (referring to the Father, Son, and Holy Spirit) from the New Testament and the Church fathers. The view that the Son was of the essence the Father, God of God—every God of every

God' was formally rectified at the first Consul of Nicaea in 325 A.D. The Holy Spirit was included at the first Consul of Constantinople (381 AD), where the relationship between the Father and Son and Holy Spirit as one substance (ousia) was formally rectified.

The definition of *ousia* from Wikipedia is as follows:

> An important philosophical and theological term, originally used in ancient Greek philosophy, then later in Christian theology. It was used by various ancient Greek philosophers, like Plato and Aristotle, as a primary designation for philosophical concepts of essence or substance.

I find nearly everything I read on the doctrine of the Trinity, as Christian theology, hard to believe. I believe if it were true, then Jesus Himself would have made statements referring to the Trinity.

In the Old Testament, it reads,

> And God said to Moses, "I AM WHO I AM." And He said, "Thus you shall say to the children of Israel, I AM has sent me to you." (Exodus 3:14)

The Bible does not teach "We as One has sent me." Isaiah 45:5 reads, "I am the Lord, and there is no other; There is no God besides Me." God has come to planet Earth many times in a glorified supernatural body. He came only once as flesh, as the only begotten Son of God in all His Glory. This would be God our Father's Glory as the Passion of Christ. Jesus is the one and true God in the flesh. Read Revelation 21:3 and Isaiah 9:6.

It is my belief that Melchizedek was a supernatural vessel or body of God. Jesus was the only—and forever only—earthly, begotten of the flesh, body of God. His reason was to offer His body as the redemption of sin and to reconcile the world back to Him through Christ Jesus. The Bible teaches this in 2 Corinthians 5:19, which reads, "That is, that God was in Christ reconciling the world to Himself, not imputing their trespasses to them, and has committed to us the word of reconciliation."

Even now, however, I can see by these statements alone that the Father, Son, and Holy Spirit was rectified by men for 345 years after the death of Christ. To my knowledge, Christ died in AD 36. These men, after 345 years, Catholic or Protestant, now are making a decision to rectify the Holy Spirit as the third person of a triune God.

A quote from Google states, "Trinity theology in most Christian faiths, the union of three Divine persons, the Father, Son, and Holy Spirit, in one God."

I cannot believe that human beings—whether they have titles such as pope, bishop, priest, preacher, evangelist, or Bible scholar—have the authority to rectify anything concerning the identity of God. Jesus the Christ is the only one who had the authority, and used it, to rectify the identity of God. In my opinion, Jesus is the identity of the one true God and Him alone, for He is the Holy Spirit. This is why we pray in the name of Jesus to identify the One true God.

I can boldly state that I will one day meet Him in Heaven as my Father. Wikipedia provides further information:

> Some Trinitarians states that the doctrine of Trinity was revealed in the New Testament times; others, that it was revealed in the Patristic period.
>
> Patristic or patrology is the study of the early Christian writers who are designated Church Fathers. The names derive from the combined forms of Latin pater and Greek pater (father). The period is generally considered to run from the end of New Testament times or end of the Apostolic Age. Nontrinitarians on the other hand, will generally state that the traditional doctrine of the Trinity did not exist until centuries after the end of the New Testament period. (We are still in the New Testament period, and will be until the return of Jesus the Christ!) Some Trinitarian's agree with this, seeing a development over time towards a true understanding of the Trinity. Trinitarian's sometime referred to Christian belief about God before the traditional statements on the Trinity as unsophisticated, "naive," or incipient Trinitarian, and that early Christians were proto-Trinitarian, partially Trinitarian', etc. Unitarians and some Trinitarians would state that this means

that those early Christians were not actually Trinitarians.

I came across an article online titled, "The Surprising Origins of the Trinity Doctrine." The article gives many Scriptures that refer to the Trinity as false doctrine. I will list only two Scriptures so that you can get an idea of what the writer may have insinuated.

> I marvel that you are turning away so soon from Him who called you in the grace of Christ, to a different gospel, which is not another; but there are some who trouble you and want to prevent the gospel of Christ. but even if we, or an angel from heaven, preach any other gospel to you then what we have preached to you, let him be accursed. (Galatians 1:6–8)
>
> But I fear, least somehow, as the serpent deceived Eve by his craftiness, so your minds may be corrupted from the simplicity that is in Christ. For if he who comes preaches another Jesus whom we have not preached, or if you receive a different spirit which you have not received, or a different gospel which you have not accepted—you may well put up with it. (2 Corinthians 11:3–4)

We may never know whether this is a false doctrine of the Trinity or a doctrine totally unrelated to the Trinity. Another issue we may never truly know is whether Paul, at this time, was preaching to the Jews or if he primarily preached to the Gentiles. Was Paul explaining to the Gentiles that they should not be deceived by any gospel other than his gospel? We may never know the answer to that, but most Trinitarian commentaries referred to false teaching to the Jews, as Paul may have been preaching in a synagogue. I personally do not believe that is the case. Based on Scripture, I can plainly see Paul in Athens, Greece, preaching to the Gentiles.

I found the following online as well. The article is "Paul and the Gentiles," written by Davina C. Lopez.

> Q. When Paul refers to his message to the Gentiles as "my gospel," can we infer that his message is distinct from that preached by Peter, James, John, etc.?
>
> A. the reader asked an important question that calls attention to the fact that there are many factors to consider when we engage biblical materials: the primary texts themselves, their ancient contexts, and their appropriation across time and cultures. In this respect, the Pauline epistles have an especially rich set of traditions with which interested readers most contend.
>
> For example, many proline concepts, such as the "law," "grace," "faith," and "works," have been shaped by long-standing debate between Protestants and Catholics and by European Christian conceptions of Jews and Judaism. It's important to note that the origins of biblical scholarship itself

are rooted in German Protestantism. As a result, there has been a scholarly tradition of separating Paul and his "Gospel" out from the Jerusalem apostles, namely Peter, James, and John. According to this tradition, Paul and the Jerusalem apostles are oppositional forces to one another, with different sources of inspiration for their theologies and actions. Herein the main difference is that the "Jerusalem gospel" requires full Torah observance by Jews and Gentiles alike, whereas the "Pauline gospel" does not require Torah observation by Gentiles. This particular reconstruction has been the subject of much debate and commentary scholarship.

There is much more to this article by Davina C. Lopez, but I will end it here.

And when James, Cephas, and John, who seem to be pillars, perceived the grace that had been given to me [meaning that they realized what Jesus Christ had given to Paul by authority—to preach the grace-age gospel, not only to Jews but to Gentiles as well. By the end of this Scripture, however, we can plainly see that Paul primarily preached to the Gentiles], they gave me and Barnabas the right hand of fellowship, that we should go to the Gentiles and they to the circumcised. (Galatians 2:9)

Many may still believe in a triune God, but I know this: I see no strong evidence of a triune God anywhere in the Bible. I believe that most Christians may put up with the belief of a triune God. I'll say this: if—and I do mean *if*—there is a Trinity, it would have to be God the Father, His earthly Tabernacle Jesus, and His Church. For we are not only His Church; we are the Saints of God, as the body of Christ. We all bear record of His truth, and we are all One in the Spirit of God. Food for thought: "Assuredly, I say to you, whatever you bind on earth will be bound in Heaven" (Matthew 18:18).

The following is the answer to a Wikipedia search of "Who used the word Trinity first?":

> The first recorded use of this Greek word in Christian theology was by Theophilus of Antioch about 170. He did not speak about the Trinity of God.

Here's Wikipedia's answer to "Who is the Father of the Trinity?":

> In Christianity the concept of God as the Father of Jesus Christ goes metaphysically through the than concept of God is the creator and Father of all people, as indicated in the apostles Creed where the expression of belief is the Father Almighty, Creator

of Heaven and Earth is immediately, but separately.

And here's Wikipedia's answer to "Who is God the Son in the Trinity?":

> God the Son (Greek: Oeocuioc) is the second person of the Trinity in Christian theology." In the Greek, the term "Son of God" is sometimes used in the Old and New Testaments of the Christian Bible to refer to those with special relationships with God.

Food for thought: While in Athens, the apostle Paul passed by the objects of worship; he even found an altar with the inscription, "To the Unknown God." From all the altars of the gods to worship, Paul proclaimed the unknown God. So I wonder: are the three persons of the said Holy Trinity a Christian theology or is it an ancient Greek and Roman theology? I know one thing for sure: whether or not we study Scripture, we will all find out, perhaps sooner than we think.

With this knowledge brought back from history, I am not convinced of a Trinity doctrine. It may or may not have ever existed, even in the very first church—Jesus and His disciples. But I am also sorry to say that I have no proof in history that it did *not* exist. Even so, I feel I must elaborate on my thoughts. We must remember that the Holy Scripture, the Bible, was not complete at that time. We, as the Church at that time, did not have the Scriptures to study to get a clear picture of what was being taught. I feel that because of the lack of true knowledge given to us in the Holy Bible today, the earthly term *Trinity* may have been taught; many Scriptures sound like contradictions, without the belief of a triune God.

A dear friend suggested that perhaps the belief in a Trinity was given to explain the unclear vision of a Heavenly mystery. That sounds like the very reason I wrote this chapter.

On the other hand, as I think back to the era of the early Church, I remember the word *Easter* in Acts 12:4 of the King James Version of the Bible, and I wonder why that word is there. I cannot see the word *Easter* appearing in any Christian Bible of any era. Why? Because I see it as an error; the word *Passover* must be used. *Passover* is used today in the New King James Version and other new translated Bibles. I believe the word Easter was deliberately placed there to draw more people into Christianity—people who, at that time, had pagan beliefs. This also forces me to think that the term *Trinity* also may have been used to draw more pagan believers into Christianity. In that era, I believe that pagans, in general, believed in more than one god. I have studied Scripture for many years and have read many articles on history concerning a Trinity. Nothing is more clear to me than the Scriptures of the Holy Bible.

Please read Acts 17:16–34. This Scripture alone led me to believe what I believe. Acts 17:23 says,

> For as I was passing through and considering the objects of your worship, I even found an altar with this inscription: To the Unknown God. Therefore, the One

> whom you worship without knowing, Him
> I proclaim to you.

I know that Paul preached to the Jews and the Gentiles. Some commentaries may claim that Paul is speaking to the Jews concerning their worshipping false idols, but I don't believe this is the case. I believe Paul is speaking to Gentiles in Athens, just as he would in Rome. At that time, these people worshipped many gods. Various Trinitarian commentaries may have a different story, and that is their God-given right to see it as they see it. Other than the Bible, the historical documents concerning this subject are vague, misleading, and unclear for a strong understanding in the knowledge of truth.

> For there are three that bear record in Heaven, the Father, the Word, and the Holy Ghost. (1 John 5:7 KJV)

As I understand Scripture, the Father is God the Almighty. The Word also is God Almighty.

> For He whom God has sent speaks the words of God for God does not give the Spirit by measure. (John 3:34)

From this Scripture, I believe we call Jesus the Word of God. But God is the Word because He spoke everything into existence by His Word. From Scripture, I can boldly state that the Son is the Father. From which Scripture is this truth known?

And without controversy great is the mystery of godliness: God was manifested in the flesh, justified in the Spirit, seen by angels, preached among the Gentiles, believed on in the world, received up in glory. (1 Timothy 3:16)

I can boldly state that Jesus is the Father because Revelation 21:3 tells us,

And I heard a loud voice from heaven saying, Behold, the Tabernacle of God is with men, and He will dwell with them, and they shall be His people. God Himself will be with them and be their God.

Jesus says in John 10:30, "I and My Father are one." Jesus didn't say, "*We* and My Father are one."

He was in the world, and the world was made by Him, and the world knew Him not. (John 1:10 KJV)

For unto us a child is born [Jesus], unto us a Son is given [this also is Jesus as the sacrifice for the remission of sin]; and the government will be upon His shoulder [this means Jesus will have authority. And His name will be called wonderful, counselor, Mighty God, Everlasting Father, Prince of Peace. (Isaiah 9:6)

The three that bear record in Heaven are the Father; His earthly Tabernacle, the Son of God (Revelation 21:3); and us, the Saints of God, His Church. Jesus said in John 20:21, "Peace to you! As the Father has sent Me, I also send you." The Father, Son, and Church are all one as the Holy Spirit of God to bear witness of His truth, the Holy Bible. I know this because we are the members of the body of Christ. If we do not preach the Word of God to a fallen world, then who will?

I pray that we all may have a renewing of the mind, in truth. I know that many in this world still do not know Him. I pray, Holy Father, that many will see the truth, and their eyes will be opened as they pray in the name of Jesus.

Jesus, the Tabernacle of God Himself, identifies the Glory of the One true God.

Praise God!

7

Worship

On the night that I completed chapter 6 of this book, I then prayed, "Lord, what should be the next topic? How will my next chapter express Your love for the Church and our love for You.

The next morning, the first word I heard in my mind was *worship*. At first, I was unsure what that meant. Then I realized it was the answer to my prayer.

Hearing the voice of God is unique. That morning, when I heard from Him, I was not quite awake. I heard Him clearly and felt Him strongly in my heart. I knew it was God, as I have heard His voice many times before. Later that morning, I thought, *Worship, worship—what shall I write concerning His love for us and our love for Him?* Then I realized that it's because of His passion of love for us that we humbly love but boldly worship Him.

We must remember this always: He loved us first, even when we were living in sin. (This truth is found in Romans 5:8.) This is why we should boldly worship God as our Father, just as Jesus taught us in Matthew 6:9–13. In Matthew 6:9, Jesus plainly says, "In this manner, therefore, pray." In verses 10 through 13, He gives us the example of how to pray to our Father in Heaven, with the famous prayer known as the Our Father or the Lord's Prayer.

Wikipedia defines *worship* as "a word often used in religion. It means to have much respect." Wikipedia also notes, "The Bible talks about people worshipping God; for example, Abraham builds an altar in Genesis 12:8."

Actually, as the Jewish religion was being established—and it took decades to complete—there was a great deal more involved in how they worshipped. In the ancient Jewish religion, they lived and worshipped God by 613 commandments—the rules of their religion. Today, because there is no temple where animals would be sacrificed as offerings to God, things are quite different in the Jewish religion. But they are still a very religious group of people, even though they do not live or worship by the 613 commandments today. This is because of the many changes in the Jewish background, such as in 70 CE, when the Romans burned and destroyed their temple in Jerusalem. This was because of their rebellion—their riots—in Jerusalem and Roman Judea in the year 66 CE. This eventually forced the Jews out of Rome and scattered them around the world (Luke 21:24).

Today, and for many years now, the Jews are returning to Israel. This was prophesied in the Bible:

> Now it shall come to pass, when all of these things come upon you, the blessings and the curse which I have set before you, and you call them to mind among all the nations where the Lord God drives you, and you return to the Lord your God and obey

His voice, according to all that I command you today, you and your children, with all your heart and with all your soul, that the Lord your God will bring you back from captivity, and have compassion on you, and gather you again from all the nations where the Lord your God has scattered you. If any of you are driven out to the furthest parts under heaven, from there the Lord your God will gather you, and from there He will bring you. Then the Lord He your God will bring you to the land which your fathers possessed, and you shall possess it. He will prosper you and multiply you more than your fathers. (Deuteronomy 30:1–5)

It seems to me that the Word of God emphasizes verse 4, as it states, "If any of you are driven out to the furthest parts under heaven, from there the Lord your God will gather you, and from there He will bring you." I wonder if verse 4 could refer to America and other countries in the Western Hemisphere. The Western Hemisphere, later known as the New World, was not discovered until centuries after the Jews had been disbursed throughout the known nations at that time. Verse 5 explains to where God is bringing them— back home to Israel. Verse 4, however, really intrigues me, especially the words "driven out to the furthest parts under heaven."

The Jews are still a very religious group of people. Even though they have suffered many hardships in their Jewish background, they use 369 *mitzvot* (commandments) today.

In the ancient Jewish religion, there were many ways to worship God.

In my opinion, practicing religion with a set of rules or commandments is not true worship. It is a form of worship, and at that time, I feel it was acceptable to God. The Jews lived under the law that was established by God Himself. We, as the church, the Saints of God, do not live under the law. Here is a biblical example of this:

> When Gallio was proconsul of Achaia, the Jews with one accord rose up against Paul and brought him to the judgment seat [the bema seat], saying, "This fellow persuades men to worship God contrary to the law." (Acts 18:12–13)

Surely at that time, the Jews must have been very upset with Paul concerning the ancient Jewish religion and the law. We must also remember that Paul was a Pharisee. This meant that Paul was very knowledgeable in the ancient laws and the practice of the Jewish religion. The Jews were upset because Paul was preaching salvation through Christ and worshipping God through the Holy Spirit. This was totally contrary to the law—the Jewish law that was given to the people by God.

As Christians, we know that the law cannot save us. No one can live a perfect life and therefore fulfill the law and be saved. Jesus the Christ is our only salvation. He fulfilled the law, but then He took sin upon Himself and paid in full for the wages of sin, which is death, when He freely gave up His life for us.

I do not believe that God created people just for many of them to die and be lost and for a few to be saved. I know what the Scriptures read; Matthew 7:14 tells us, "Because narrow is the gate and difficult is the way which leads to life, and there are few who find it."

My thoughts are of the people of the world, starting from the time of Adam and Eve, mainly after they had fallen to sin by disobeying God. Of course, this led to the death of Abel. When Cain killed Abel, it was the first blood shed into the pure, clean soil of the Earth. All things changed. Thorns and countless varieties of worthless weeds began to grow, as sin grew rapidly in the world. There was no guidance in the light of Jesus Christ, but I believe there was a way of salvation.

At the time of Noah, God was going to destroy Noah and his family and everyone on the planet.

> So the Lord said, "I will destroy man I have created from the face of the earth, both man and beast, creeping things and birds of the air, for I am sorry that I have made them." But Noah found grace in the eyes of the Lord. (Genesis 6:7–8)

The ark that Noah built was a way of salvation for anyone who would have boarded it. Even after the great flood, sin grew rapidly in the world and has continued. From the time of Noah and the great flood and up to this very day, the world has had many cultures and communities. Every culture that gathered as a community, or tribe, as a way of life had laws by which they abided. Consider Native

Americans, for example. These are very spiritual people. I might assume that all pagan religions of the early ages had spiritual guidance of some kind and a law of some kind to follow. Were these laws given to them by God, as they were to the Jewish people who were once of pagan dissent? I don't think so. Their laws were from the minds of human men, created in the image of God.

Of course, this image was not in full but dimmed somewhat in the darkness of this sinful world. Even so, the Bible states, "If you then, being evil, know how to give good gifts unto your children, how much more will your Father who is in Heaven give good things to those who ask Him!" (Matthew 7:11).

Again, consider Native Americans and other people who live outside the knowledge of Jesus (this would have been many years ago but perhaps includes some primitive people in remote places of the world today) Living under a tribal law, what would be their chances of being saved? Did God create them just to die and go to hell? I don't think so.

> For as many as have sinned without law will also perish without law, and as many as have sinned in the law will be judged by the law (for not the hearers of the law are just in the sight of God, but the doers of the law will be justified; for when Gentiles, who do not have the law, by nature do the things in the law, *these*, although not having the law, are a law to themselves, who show the work of the law written in their hearts, their conscience also being witness, and

between themselves their thoughts accusing
or else excusing them) in the day when *God
will judge the secrets of men by Jesus Christ,*
according to my gospel. (Romans 2:12–16,
italics added)

I believe that according to that time and according
to Scripture, every knee shall bow. I believe every man
and woman descended from Adam and Eve and will stand
before Jesus the Christ for judgment. Whether from the
Old Testament, living under the law, or any other time
prior to the Old Testament, the atonement of their sins
will be justified and reconciled of God through the death
of Jesus Christ, our Savior, the Tabernacle of God Himself
(Revelation 21:3).

I believe that in all of God's creation of men and women,
no matter what era, salvation was offered to them. I believe
it was by the innocent bloodshed of Christ, which fell into
the sinful, bloodshed soil of this earth, that Jesus paid the
price for sin. Jesus made preparation to make amends for a
wrong one has done. Jesus Christ made the reconciliation
of God and humankind. We must fully understand the
Scripture; Jesus was the Tabernacle of God Himself, and He
was living in the world with us, as God in a flesh vessel—the
only begotten of flesh, Tabernacle of God, ever (Revelation
21:3) in any Christian Bible!

I believe true worship comes from the innermost part
of a person—the soul of humankind. I have no doubt that
from our minds, our wills, and our emotions, there is a
record of our lives. Our choices in life are all recorded. This
record of life indicates the true identity of our spirits, which

leads us to destruction or salvation through Christ Jesus. Someone may think that God does not keep records because He is all-forgiving! But if our minds, our wills, and our emotions are of this world, then we are of this world and not of God. Our names will not be found in the book of life. There has to be a record of life; even in this world, we have the knowledge of history.

When God breathed into Adam's nostrils and he became a living soul, his history began! And it wasn't only for Adam but for every living thing on this planet. The history of life is recorded. As for humankind, we will be judged in one way or another. I say this because of the judgment seat, or bema seat, of Christ for the Saints of God (Romans 14:10–12). As for those who were lost, their history will be brought up at the white-throne judgment (Revelation 20:11–15).

As the church, the Saints of God, we live in a new era—the New Testament, the grace age. Our worship comes from the innermost part of our beings, the soul, the identity of our spirits. Remember:

> But the hour is coming, and now is, when the true worshipers will worship the Father in spirit and truth; for the Father is seeking such to worship Him. God is Spirit, and those who worship Him must worship Him in spirit and truth. (John 4:23–24)

John 4:21 says that Jesus said to her, "Woman, believe Me, the hour is coming when you will neither on this mountain, nor in Jerusalem, worship the Father." In my opinion, Jesus is plainly telling this woman there will be an end to all religions. She was a Gentile; Jerusalem is of the Jewish faith. But in verse 22, Jesus makes it clear that at that time, true worship and salvation was of the Jews. In verse 23, however, He is clearly speaking of a new era. As Jesus said, "But the hour is coming, and now is, when the true worshipers will worship the Father in spirit and truth; For the Father is seeking such to worship Him." It is my opinion that Jesus is making it clear that this worship is completely different from the type of worship of the Old Testament.

Remember that Jesus was born and raised in the worship of the Jewish faith. Also remember that this was the Old Testament, the law and traditions, given only to God's chosen people, the Jews. Christ Jesus, the Messiah, came out from among the Jewish faith for our salvation. No one at that time, I believe, realized the change that Jesus brought as a New Testament. We contain this worship is of His Spirit inside our bodies, or our temples of the Holy Spirit. Jesus makes it very clear to me when He says, "God is a Spirit, and those who worship Him must worship Him in spirit and truth" (John 4:24).

Second Corinthians 3:1–18 explains to me the truth of the new worship in the New Testament:

> Do we begin again to commend ourselves? Or do we need, as some others, the epistles of commendation to you or letters of commendation from you? You are our epistle written in our hearts, know and read by all men; clearly you are an epistle of Christ, ministered by us, written not with ink but by the Spirit of the living God, not

on tablets of stone but on tablets of flesh, that is, of the heart.

And we had such trust through Christ toward God. Not that we are sufficient of ourselves to think of anything as being from ourselves, but our sufficiency is from God, who also made us sufficient as ministers of the new covenant, not of the letter [the law] but of the Spirit; for the letter kills, but the Spirit gives life.

But if the ministry of death, written and engraved on stones, was glorious, so that the children of Israel could not look steadily at the face of Moses because of the glory of his countenance, which glory was passing away, how will the ministry of the Spirit not be more glorious? For if the ministry of [the law] condemnation had glory, the ministry of righteousness exceeds much more in glory. For even what was made glorious had no glory in this respect, because of the glory that excels. For if what is passing away was glorious [Old Testament], what remains is much more glorious [New Testament].

Therefore, since we have such hope, we use great boldness of speech—unlike Moses, who put a veil over his face so that the children of Israel could not look steadily at the end of what was passing away. But their minds were blinded. For until this day the same veil remains unlifted in the reading of the Old Testament, because the veil is taken away in Christ. But even to this day, when Moses is read, a veil lies on their heart. Nevertheless when one turns to the Lord, the veil is taken away. Now the Lord is the Spirit; and where the Spirit of the Lord is, there is liberty. But we all, with unveiled face, beholding as in a mirror of the glory of the Lord, are being transformed into the same image from glory to glory, just as by the Spirit of the Lord.

This Scripture in 2 Corinthians gives me a greater knowledge of understanding as to why my God endured the passion of Christ. The love of God has endured and conquered all things of this world. He conquered sin and death for the love of His Church, the Saints of God. Whether we are Jew or Gentile, that blinding veil must be lifted to see His Glory. The only way this can happen is by accepting Jesus, the love of God, the passion of Christ.

I pray you will understand and hear my next words with an open heart: If yesterday is gone, and tomorrow is of no promise, then today is the only day of life. Have you ever heard the expression, "Here today, gone tomorrow"? That's a very true statement! We may never know *which* tomorrow, for it could be today. I pray that you know where you are today.

We are in the only physical day of life here on earth. Yesterday is gone, so we are not there. Tomorrow may not come; we may never be there. That brings us to the reality in the physical world of today; it is the only day of life. I know this is a literal and physical fact, and I cannot help but say that every day is a day of salvation and a day of worship.

As the Saints of God, the Church, we can freely worship God. Because His Spirit lives within us, we have no rules or regulations. We have His love, and we give love back by free worship in return, not by commandments, rules, laws, or regulations. True worship is given to us by the Spirit of God. True worship is love. God taught us this love by the passion of Christ, His Son (John 3:16), the Tabernacle of God Himself (Revelation 21:3).

In my opinion, it does not matter how we see Jesus—as the Son of God or the Tabernacle of God Himself. What truly matters is knowing that Jesus is our only salvation. The Bible makes it very clear: there is only one God, one faith, one baptism.

> One Lord, one faith, one baptism, one God and Father of all, who is above all, and through all, and in you all. (Ephesians 4:5–6)

As Christians in the body of Christ, we believe in only one God. Because of the passion of Christ, the greatest statement of love ever expressed to the world, and knowing it was my God doing it for me, I can't help but see One God—*only*! If I were to say that Jesus was the second person, as an entity, of the Holy Trinity, I would lose my understanding of faith in an all-merciful God, an all-loving God, but most of all, an Almighty God. How could I see Him as an Almighty God if He needed the help of a second and third person, as other entities in a Holy Trinity? I never saw it or understood it, even when I was a Catholic or a Baptist. But I was told that was quite all right because it was a God thing, and we may never understand it until the day we meet Him in Heaven. With all the knowledge of history and Scripture that I have mustered over the past forty years, however, I just cannot see that as Christian theology.

On the other hand, knowing my God as I do—I know His love for His creation; that He is the Creator of all; that my heavenly Father came here as the Son of God in all His Glory, our Father's Glory; that Jesus was the servant as the Tabernacle of God Himself; and that He, the Creator of all, came to endure the passion of Christ as the servant—then He is my God, all in all, the One and Only. This I know and believe.

Praise God, our Father!

8

Who Was Saul of Tarsus?

In my understanding of Scripture, Saul was a man who loved God very much. Saul was a Pharisee, which meant he was well educated in the ancient laws and traditions of the Jewish religion. Saul believed that what he did—helping to destroy the movement of Christianity—was the will of God, mainly because of the 613 commandments, or laws, that would be practiced in his Jewish religion.

Saul profited well in his religion. Because of his knowledge and the love he had for his forefathers, Saul felt very secure in his Jewish religion; he was truly a religious fanatic. As I read Scripture, I can see Saul diligently seeking my brothers and sisters in Christ for their imprisonment or death. I see him no different from Saddam Hussein or Osama bin Laden or perhaps any high-ranking leader of ISIS.

Though I can see him as a religious fanatic who killed many, simply because they did not believe in or understand the existence of God as he did, I can plainly see, by Scripture, that God had a great plan for Saul. I can clearly see, by all Scripture, that the Jewish worshipers, such as Saul and the Disciples of Christ, either did not know or didn't fully understand the changes concerning the development of the

Church Age. These changes are indeed great changes for the Jewish worshipers such as Saul, and the Grace Age Disciples of Christ. It is clearly my understanding, by all Scripture, that the Old Testament Jews and the New Testament Grace Age Disciples of Christ did not fully understand what was taking place.

Many of the New Testament Disciples knew Jesus was the Son of God, as their Messiah, but most Jews, including Saul, did not believe. When Saul met Jesus after His death, burial, and resurrection, Saul met Him in the Spirit, as the One and True God he claimed to know. When Saul met Christ on the road to Damascus, his mind was renewed. Though Saul was a Jew and a Pharisee, he no longer worshipped God with religion concerning the law. He now worshipped God from his heart, from the grace he received from the passion of Christ.

Saul finally met the God he loved and then lived in a relationship with Him. Because of the passion of love, known as the passion of Christ, we all may see Him as the One and True God, as He offers us His loving Grace.

Saul, or Paul, as our Lord Jesus named him, was born sometime around the year 5 CE in the city of Tarsus in Cilicia, which is now modern-day Turkey. Saul was born of Jewish parents who possessed Roman citizenship, a privilege that Saul himself would possess.

Many believe that Saul's family moved to Jerusalem sometime between the years 15 and 20 CE. This is when, it is believed, Saul began the study of the Hebrew Scriptures in Jerusalem. Saul was a very dedicated young man, under the care and teachings of a famous Rabbi at that time named

Gamaliel. This Rabbi Gamaliel led Saul into a very deep and thorough study of the ancient Jewish laws.

There is some debate over whether Saul was raised in Jerusalem or in Tarsus, where he was born. Regardless of the facts, Paul indicates, by his own words, the truth of where he was raised.

> I am indeed a Jew, born in Tarsus of Cilicia, but brought up in this city [Jerusalem] at the feet of Gamaliel, taught accordingly to the strictness of our fathers' law, and were zealous towards God as you all are today. (Acts 22:3)

Also consider that Paul or Saul stated in Acts 23:16–17 that Saul and his entire immediate family most likely moved to Jerusalem when Saul and his siblings were very young. Read Acts 23:16–17, and realize his name is no longer Saul but Paul (changed by our Lord Jesus). This had to be many years after his studies of the Hebrew law and the Jewish religion.

When we read of the death of Stephen, a disciple of Christ, in Acts 7:54–60, we will learn the details of his so-called trial and execution. Saul stood there as a witness. But in Acts 8:1–3, we learn that Saul consented to the death of Stephen and was ready and willing to persecute many members of the Church in Jerusalem—or anywhere else he could find them.

In the book of Acts 9:1–20, we learn that Saul had persecuted the Church but then was blinded on the road to Damascus. We learn in Acts 9:10 that the Lord spoke with Ananias, saying, "Arise and go to the street called Straight, and inquire at the house of Judah's for one called Saul of Tarsus, for behold, he is praying." Then, Acts 9:17–19 explains that Ananias laid hands on him so that he regained his sight, and he was filled with the Holy Spirit and was baptized. Acts 9:20 states that immediately, he preached in the synagogues that Christ is the Son of God.

Saul, a man raised as a Jew and having a very high education in the ancient laws of the Jewish religion, taught by the famous Rabbi Gamaliel, now had a very serious change of heart. Saul was very strong in his Jewish background and in the beliefs from the forefathers of his Jewish religion. Saul did not know he was living in a time of change. Saul did not know that in the hallway of the great Jewish Temple of Jerusalem, the doorway to Heaven would shut, and another, by the grace of God, would open.

Saul became a changed man. Why? It was time for a change—the big change from religion back to relationship; from a knowledge of the One and True God, to the intimate knowledge in a relationship with the One and True God, as Adam and Eve had before they fell into sin.

I believe that the Old Testament Saints, especially as prophets, had great faith, probably greater faith than many of us Christians have today. This is not to say that modern Christians don't have great faith, but I can somehow feel that faith of Shadrach, Meshach, and Abednego. I can almost see them walking into that fiery furnace. I can almost feel their thoughts of a joyful ending—not the thought that they would still be alive but the pleasure in their faith that they did not bow down to another god.

Many others display great faith in the Old Testament, but the point is that Saul, a man who was raised in the Old Testament and lived by the traditions of Jewish faith, now met God for the first time. Saul lived in a time of change, from Old to New. He had become a new man, Paul—a new creature in Christ, as a disciple of Christ.

We must remember that Paul was very educated in the Jewish religion and the ancient laws. So, if he was so educated in the knowledge of the Torah and the ancient laws of the Jewish faith, how did he *not* know that Jesus was the Messiah? My own experience in reading and studying Scripture tells me that before Paul met Christ on the road to Damascus, he was not filled with the Holy Spirit. Rather, he was filled with the knowledge of Scripture from the Torah and the Jewish ancient laws that he was taught by the most-famous Rabbi Gamaliel. This clearly means that he was taught traditions and beliefs of another man's work. He didn't find truth for himself; he clearly followed the beliefs of another. Paul felt he was secure in this man's teachings because he was such a famous Rabbi at that time.

I am very troubled to say this, but I see the life of Paul as no different from the lives of the many Christians of today. We have many denominations of Christianity, which we all call *religions*. I will give you an example. Someone may be asked, "What religion are you?" The answer may be "I am a Catholic," or "I'm a Baptist," or "I'm Pentecostal," and so on! The truth is that in many cases, we were taught what to believe long before we were ever taught anything about the Holy Spirit dwelling in us.

In comparing the life of Paul to our lives today, I see very little difference. First of all, Paul never met Jesus in the flesh, and neither do we today. Paul met Jesus the Christ in the spirit—the same as we do today. Paul least expected and was totally unaware of what would happen to him on the road to Damascus. This is the same for many of us today in our travels in life.

I could say many thing about the Apostle Paul, but I feel the greatest thing about him is the Glory of God. God took a spiritually blind man and physically blinded him on the road to Damascus, which opened his eyes and his heart to the reality of the one and true God. Paul no longer gave glory to the traditions of men by his religious beliefs. Paul no longer lived that life. Paul now lived in the Glory of God, as the Glory of God's Church, the body of Christ, for the Glory of God—the same as we do today. What a great testimony. Praise God!

9

From Carnal Language to Spiritual Knowledge

T he Old Testament Saints had great faith. Even so, they did not have what we have as Christians today. We have the Holy Spirit dwelling in us, as the temple of God. As Christians, we also have the written Word of God, the Holy Bible. Please think about this, spiritually and deeply, as I quote John 17:21–23:

> That they all be one, as you, Father, or in Me, and I in You; that they also may be one in Us, that the world may believe that You sent Me. and the glory which you have gave me I have given them that they may be one just as we are one: "I in them, and You in Me; that they may be made perfect in one, and that the world may know that You have sent Me, and have loved them as you loved Me."

This Scripture, in my opinion, relates to the passion of Christ. The Scriptures speak of one Spirit, the Holy Spirit,

God our Father. John 17:22 speaks of the Glory of God that was given to Jesus. Then Jesus states that He has given it to us to be as one, just as they are one as Father and Son. The Bible does not contradict itself. Therefore, when it sounds like a contradiction, it is our lack of understanding of the Scripture.

Isaiah 42:8 states, "I am the Lord, that is My name; and My glory I will not give to another." It is my belief, because of the Scriptures, that Jesus the Christ (or as Revelation 21:3 refers to Him, the Tabernacle of God Himself) is showing the world and the now-known ministry of the Church, in the written Word of God, all His love and His Glory as the Son of God. This He freely gave to us by His death on the cross, which made us one in Christ, as Christ is one in the Father.

In my opinion, it is all about one Spirit, the Holy Spirit. Therefore, we are His Glory as the Church, the body of Christ. Second Corinthians 5:19 plainly states, "That is, that God was in Christ reconciling the world to Himself, not imputing their trespasses to them, and has committed to us the word of reconciliation." We may learn that God uses His creation of man (humankind) to teach us all things. Christ was human as the man Jesus, teaching us earthly and heavenly things by His earthly ministry.

Also keep in mind that humankind, the creation of God that He loved so much, was given the Spiritual authority to record His precious Word by writing the Holy Bible. Jesus said, "Greater love has no one than this, than to lay down one's life for his friends" (John 15:13). Jesus also said, "No longer do I call you servants, for a servant does not know what his master is doing; but I have called you friends, for all things that I heard from My Father I have made known to you" (John 15:15).

Keep in mind that as carnal understanding in the physical world, Jesus was conceived in His mother Mary by the Word of God. Also, we *must* keep in mind that Jesus the Christ, by Spiritual knowledge from the Word of God, was God Himself, by the knowledge of Scripture: Revelation 21:3, 1 Timothy 3:16, John 1:14, and John 1:10, just to mention a few.

Most important, because of carnal and spiritual understanding, we must realize the truth of what the Scriptures teach us. For example, what if someone asked you, "How can I believe that the Bible is truth when humankind wrote it?" My answer would be, "How can we not believe it?" When we are equipped with the knowledge of Scripture, we can clearly see that God uses humankind for all things, even to go to the cross!

It is also my opinion that in Luke 22:27, Jesus explains that He is greater than what He seems to be. He asks the question: "For who is greater, he who sits at the table, or he who serves? Is it not he who sits at the table? Yet I am among you as One who serves."

Then, in Luke 22:28–30, Jesus goes on to speak about His kingdom.

I see this so plainly in all Scripture. Our heavenly Father stepped down from His throne and came to His creation as man in all His glory, as Jesus, or as the Christ, the Tabernacle of God Himself, for the remission of sin. God was in Christ, reconciling the world to Himself. This is my God, the Almighty, the all-merciful and all-loving God, who loved His creation so much that He came as the creation of man, as the Son of God, the only begotten of the Father. He suffered the passion of Christ; then He was nailed to a cross and gave up His earthly life as flesh, as the ultimate sacrifice for the forgiveness of sin.

> For God so loved the world that He gave His only begotten son, that whoever believes in Him should not perish but have everlasting life. (John 3:16)

I love that Scripture, whether it is understood by carnal understanding or the spiritual understanding in all Scripture. We know the truth of it and understand it is speaking of the passion of Christ. Many of us may not realize, however, that Christ is not Jesus's surname. It is His title as the anointed One, which means He was God in the flesh (Revelation 21:3), the Tabernacle of God Himself. The man Jesus was sent for our salvation!

I don't understand how anyone can understand Scripture if they don't use Scripture to explain Scripture. I will give a list of Scripture that explain the Almighty, all-loving, and all-merciful God, with a passion of love for His creation and how He has reclaimed His creation by the redemption of sin.

1. "They shall call His name Immanuel, which is translated, God with us" (Matthew 1:23). He was sent!
2. "I am the Lord, and there is no other; there is no God besides Me" (Isaiah 45:5). This same Scripture in the King James Version reads, "There is no God beside me," which would mean next to Him—to His left or His right. Whether it's *besides* or *beside*

makes no difference to me because the Bible makes a clear point—there is only one God, and He was sent!

3. "Now see that, I even I, am He, and there is no God besides me" (Deuteronomy 32:39). He was sent!

4. "And without controversy great is the mystery of godliness; God was manifested in the flesh, justified in the Spirit, seen by Angels, preached among the Gentiles, believed on in the world, received up in glory" (1 Timothy 3:16). He was sent!

5. "And the Word became flesh and dwelt among us, and we beheld His glory, the glory as of the only begotten of the Father, full of grace and truth" (John 1:14). I must confirm who the Word is who became flesh and dwelt among us. Of course, it was God Almighty. The Bible clearly tells us that He is the Creator of all, and that He creates by His Word. He spoke everything into existence. But who brought us His Word? Of course it was Jesus, the only begotten of the flesh, the Son of God. How do I know this? By the Scripture, of course. (He was sent!)

6. "For He whom God has sent speaks the words of God, for God does not give the Spirit by measure" (John 3:34). Jesus was conceived by the Word of God in the Virgin Mary and born like any other human being on this planet. But He was not like any other human being. He was the anointed One, the Christ, who would be filled with the fullness of the Spirit of God. John 4:24 states, "God is Spirit." This is in any Christian Bible. From the

Scripture—for God does not give the Spirit by measure—I believe it means that Jesus was God, the Almighty Holy Spirit, in that flesh, that human body. (He was sent!)

7. "For I want you to know what a great conflict I have for you and those in Laodicea, and for as many as have not seen my face in the flesh, that their hearts may be encouraged, being knit together in love, and attaining to all riches of the full assurance of understanding, to the knowledge of the mystery of God, both of the Father and of Christ" (Colossians 2:1–2). Christ the anointed one—He was sent!

8. "Beware lest anyone cheat you through philosophy and empty deceit, according to the traditions of men, according to the basic principles of the world, and not according to Christ. For in Him dwells all the fullness of the Godhead bodily" (Colossians 2:8–9). Sounds to me like this Scripture may be warning us of carnal understanding but encouraging us to find the Spiritual knowledge through Christ. (He was sent!)

9. "And I heard a loud voice from heaven saying, Behold, the tabernacle of God is with men, and He will dwell with them, and they shall be His people. God Himself will be with them and be their God" (Revelation 21:3). He was sent!

10. "For unto us a child is born, unto us a Son is given; And the government will be upon His shoulder. And His name will be called Wonderful, Counselor, Mighty God, Everlasting Father, Prince of peace" (Isaiah 9:6). He was sent!

Jesus said in John 20:21, "Peace to you! As the Father has sent Me, I also send you." Notice in this verse that Jesus states, (the) Father, *not my father*! Why? In my opinion, it is because He is speaking of the One and Only Almighty Holy Spirit, His fullness in Spirit.

In the King James Version, John 20:21 uses "My Father," but it makes no difference because God is His Father by creation. Yes! You read it correctly. Jesus the man was conceived in His earthly mother by the Word of God. But it makes more biblical sense to me when Jesus refers to (the) Father, because I see it as His fullness of the Holy Spirit.

> And when He had said this, He breathed on them, and said to them, received the Holy Spirit. (John 20:22)

By the spiritual understanding of the carnal language of this Scripture, I can clearly see that God is offering us His Spirit, as believers, for the Glory of His Church.

> If you forgive the sins of any, they are forgiven them; if you retain the sins of any, they are retained. (John 20:23)

I believe the reason Jesus said these things is that He is the anointed One, filled with the fullness of the Holy Spirit. Therefore, He has given us, as the Church, the authority, as ambassadors of Christ, to witness the truth of His Word. He was sent—as the Son of God, as the Glory of God, for the Glory of His Church.

> For there are three that bear witness in
> Heaven: the Father, the Word, and the Holy
> Spirit; and these three are one. (1 John 5:7)

It doesn't matter how it is translated. What matters is that we know who we are as the Church.

The most important thing I have learned from all Scripture is that there are three who are One in Spirit. The Scriptures are clear on the facts of how and why. These three are—without any doubt in all Scripture—the Father, as the Almighty Holy Spirit; the Son, as the Spirit of God on earth in human form, as the beginning of the church, the body of Christ; and then us, as His Church on earth in human form, as the expression of the Holy Spirit living in the world today, as the Spirit of God. In the truth of it all, "So then faith comes by hearing, and hearing by the Word of God" (Romans 10:17). If we, as the church, the ambassadors of Christ, will not preach the Word of God to a dying and fallen world, then who will? We, as the Church, bear witness to the truth of the Word of God.

Do we truly understand how important it is for us to be of the body of Christ? Do we understand that we, as the Church of God, will one day judge the world and angels?

> Do you not know that the saints will judge
> the world? And if the world will be judged
> by you, are you unworthy to judge the
> smallest matters? Do you not know that we
> shall judge angels? How much more, things
> that pertain to this life? (1 Corinthians
> 6:2–3)

Can we realize that God has a plan for each and every one of us—to be a part of the body of Christ? I believe this is why God Himself gave us all the love, passion, and mercy within Him at the cross, so that none might perish. He gave us all a way of salvation through His passion as Christ. His love and His Glory were freely offered to us by His only earthly Tabernacle, as the Son of God, Jesus the Christ, the King of Kings and Lord of Lords. God truly is an awesome God with a love beyond measure. For the passion of Christ was above all and beyond any measure of comprehension or understanding of His expressions, by the actions and emotions of love. This is my God. He truly is Almighty and all in all.

Praise be to God!

10

Closing Words from My Heart

I pray that you will understand with your heart and mind what I believe to be the truth from the knowledge of Scripture quoted in this book. God has allowed me to write not only this book but my first two books as well. The Word of God, the Holy Bible, is the Glorified truth. God is truly the author of all things, as we can detect by these Bible quotes:

> I am the Alpha and the Omega, the beginning and the end, the first and the last. (Revelation 22:13)
>
> Before the mountains were brought forth, Or, ever you had formed the earth and the world, Even, from everlasting to everlasting, you are God. (Psalm 90:2)

These Scriptures tell me that nothing in this world can exist or be known to us, except first by the significance of God.

The definition of *significance* found in a Google search reads, "the quality of being worthy of attention; importance. Statistics of, or relating to observations that are unlikely to occur by chance, and that therefore indicate a systematic cause."

I'll give you my definition of significance: the will of God, as His Word is spoken, which brings forth the evidence of what is in the mind of God, supernaturally formed by His Holy Spirit and brought to this physical world, as we may know it.

Please think deeply on what I am about to say. Gather your thoughts with the knowledge of Scripture as the forgiveness of God, paid in full by the passion of Christ. I will say this in truth about myself: I am not a righteous man; I'm a man only. Yet now, I am a man who yearns for the righteousness of God. With the knowledge of the passion of Christ deep within my natural spirit, and my presence in the Holy Spirit as well, I am sometimes in spiritual warfare because of the natural causes in this life.

> For we do not wrestle against flesh and
> blood, but against principalities, against
> powers, against the rulers of the darkness of
> this age, against spiritual host of wickedness
> in the heavenly places. (Ephesians 6:12)

The Scriptures go on to tell us we must put on the whole armor of God, that we must stand strong in the truth of the Word of God and, in all His righteousness, be prepared with the knowledge of His gospel. This will give us great faith, strong enough to bear against the craftiness of the wickedness of Satan. We will then know our salvation from the Holy Spirit as the passion of Christ, which is the knowledge of the Word of God. We will constantly pray for one another as the Saints of God and boldly speak the mysteries of the gospel, for we are truly ambassadors of Christ. If we seek knowledge and receive revelation from Christ, we will speak boldly. There is no choice; it is a reality!

Surely there are many questions with regard to knowledge in this life received from the Word of God. Some answers lead to disputes among us. This is quite understandable to me because we are at different levels of understanding, whether from the Word of God or in life itself.

The truth is this: there are many denominations of Christianity. Therefore, there are many different understandings of Scripture, taught by each individual denomination. I don't have a problem with that because Matthew 18:20 states, "For where two or three are gathered together in my name, there am I in the midst of them."

> For just as the body is one and has many members, and all the members of the body, though many, are one body, so it is with Christ. (1 Corinthians 12:12)
>
> For as we have many members in one body, but all members do not have the same function, so we, being many, are one body in Christ, and individually members of one another. Having then gifts differing according to the grace that is giving to us, let us use them: if prophecy, let us prophecy in proportion to our faith; or ministry, let us use it in our ministering; he who teaches, in teaching; he who exhorts, in exhortation; he who gives, with liberality; he who leads,

> with diligence; he who shows mercy, with
> cheerfulness. Let love be without hypocrisy.
> Abhor [or hate] what is evil. Cling to what
> is good. Be kindly affectionate to one
> another with brotherly love, in honor giving
> preference to one another. (Romans 12:4–10)

With this knowledge of Scripture, I can understand why I do not fully agree or disagree with any Christian denomination. We all have truth, and we all have an era. I do not say this to discredit any denomination. I have respect and love for them all. Through the many years of my searching for the truth about God, I have been affiliated with many denominations. I have learned great things from each one of them. This is why I know we all need Jesus, for He is the body and the Church, and we are the many members, no matter how great or small.

I say this in truth with a passion of concern for the many souls of this world. God does not want anyone to perish or to be lost but for all to be saved. The truth of this is given in 1 Timothy 2:3–4: "For this is good and acceptable in the sight of God our Savior, who desires all men to be saved and to come to the knowledge of the truth."

I cannot claim that I have total truth or that I have all understanding of Scripture. If I did, I would be a complete liar. But I can strongly state this in truth: I believe every word I write or preach is truth, and I will stand before God with great boldness of truth! God Himself has made me the man I am today.

Praise be to my Lord, my God, my Savior, in Jesus's name!

Printed in the United States
By Bookmasters